D0729542

BACK TO
BASICS
IN CHURCH GROWTH

Donald McGavran
& Win Arn

Tyndale House
Publishers, Inc.
Wheaton, Illinois

Library of Congress Catalog Card Number 80-53244
ISBN 0-8423-0116-X, paper
Copyright © 1981 by Donald McGavran and Winfield Arn.
All rights reserved.

Second printing, April 1984
Printed in the United States of America

Contents

Introduction

We live in a pluralistic world. This commonplace
excites no comment today. Everyone knows it.
Yet Christians believe that pluralism in no way
cancels the Lordship of Christ. It is of this
pluralistic world that Jesus is Lord. In *this* world
every knee shall bow and every tongue confess
that Jesus Christ is Lord to the glory of the
Father. What does it mean for Jesus to be Lord
in a world which is increasingly accepted as
essentially pluralistic? This book will explore this
white-hot topic.

At the outset, we point out that the conviction
that Jesus rules over pluralism is being steadily
eroded by the main currents of modern life. The
media neither believe it nor announce it. The
science of anthropology, proclaiming all cultures
equally good, actively attacks it. The minorities
which multiply across the land demonstrate very
different life styles and each claims an inalienable
right to live its own. A pluralism in which no
one rules is what the modern world appears to
believe in. To many, if not to most Americans,
that is the situation. Let us elaborate.

The six continents with their four billion
residents (soon to become six billion) are in
reality a tremendous mosaic. Their unity consists
merely in the fact that all men are passengers on
Planet Earth and no one can get off. They have
to live together. Consequently they like the
notion that thousands of different life styles must

somehow or other get along with each other.
Each piece of the mosaic is to be left free to do
its own thing. No majority should force other
pieces of the mosaic to live as it thinks right.
Neither should any minority. This is a pluralistic
world.

Christians subscribe to this doctrine, which has
burst on the Western world in the last thirty
years, but a bit uneasily. We believe it, but with
some qualifications and reservations. Apparently
some cultural ways are going to be imposed on
everyone. All alike will have to give up thinking
in quarts and miles and begin to think in liters
and kilometers. All alike will be molded by
educational standards laid down by the State.
Many Christians are unhappy at this last one.
They see their children being conformed to the
image which pleases a secular state and a dollar-
dominated television industry. But so far Christians have done very little to combat this
manifestation of the pluralistic world.

Seemingly in this pluralistic world we can force
the metric system, secular educational standards,
health and traffic rules on all peoples, but cannot
force on anyone Christian standards concerning
sex, brotherhood, or the worship of God.
Individuals may or may not believe what the
Bible lays down as absolute truth. We are not
commending all this. We are simply describing
the contemporary situation.

In this permissive atmosphere how can
certainty survive? What happens to the Lordship
of Christ? The new orthodoxy of the pluralistic
world forces on everyone an official dogma of
secular society: that in measurable matters—the
world of sense and substance—through a process
of consensus, uniform standards and values may
be imposed, but in absolute matters each person

must be left free to follow his own desires and form his own guesses as to what truth is. Is man free or an automaton? Is this a mechanistic world closed to all free will? Does everything have an antecedent material cause? Is there a spirit world? Is there life after death or is death the end? Is the universe a vast impersonal process or is a personal Being behind it all? In these matters, the pluralistic world seems to say, "Everyone speculates as he wishes. Each of us forms his habits, chooses his associates, and adopts rules of life in conformity with his speculations. There is no absolute truth, no one way which pleases God." For many Christians, certainty is one of the casualties of their sudden realization that people are all residents in one vast apartment house with many different life styles and must get along together. Such Christians come to believe that truth is only "what is true for me." Exactly the opposite may be "true" for you.

We have been describing action in Western democracies. In totalitarian states (whether Marxist or Moslem) the situation is otherwise. There the beliefs of the party in control, even if it is a minority, are forced on everyone. Minorities in many nations firmly believe that the only way to a just society is through the dictatorship of the proletariat. That is one of the enduring springs of action in great sections of the Global Village.

This multifaceted world is complex and of fascinating interest. We and our grandchildren—unless a world government comes in by conquest—will be struggling with the implications of freedom, justice, and truth in a world where the ways of thousands of other segments of society impinge upon us. As I write, the Vietnamese decision to make life miserable for the two million citizens of Chinese origin and drive them out of the land is gravely interfering with the life of Hong Kong, Singapore, Malaysia, the United States, and other lands. Yet no one says to Vietnam, "The world community will not allow you to do this." Rather, Vietnam practices genocide before our eyes, a million die, and the rest of the world, groaning and complaining, absorbs a million boat people.

This volume on the convictional foundations of church growth cannot treat the pluralistic problem in its broad aspects. We confine ourselves to the threat it poses to Christian certainty. Since the foundation of the pluralistic order is the conviction that each life style is about equally valid, Christians find their own children and themselves drifting almost unconsciously toward relativistic religion. This holds that no one has *The Truth*. All religions and ideologies are partly true and partly false. People say, "You know a part of the truth. So do I. Let's get together and dialogue. Perhaps we shall together arrive at a truer concept of reality. Jesus Christ was a very great man, but then so were Gautama, Krishna, Confucius, and Marx. Who knows? Eastern cults and Western scientism may be right."

This climate of thought is the antithesis of that of the New Testament church—indeed, of the entire biblical revelation. Yet church growth today must proceed in this pluralistic milieu. What is the right attitude toward this influential contemporary dogma? What light does the Bible itself shed on this fashionable doctrine?

Against this background, the thesis of this book may now be stated. We hold that the growth of the church is not dependent primarily on methods which will operate in any organization and on any theory of eternal truth. Rather, church growth depends on conviction that the biblical revelation has been given by God and that, in the absolute matters concerning man and God, *God has revealed himself and his perfect will authoritatively. Christians in this century or any other, this land or any other, may confidently go forward, knowing that they are basing their actions on unchanging truth.*

It is essential to remember that while Christians base their actions on God's truth, the truth which the Bible reveals is not fully exemplified in any empirical church. The early church in Jerusalem did not fully exemplify it. They "spake the Word to none but Jews." The church in its days of greatest purity and glory did not fully exemplify it. The One Way is never what any given church does. Its rituals, customs, hymns, and doctrines are all man-made and imperfect. No culture is fully Christian. However, empirical churches which intend to practice what God has revealed are much closer to the divine model than others. The churches of the Reformation were much closer than the corrupt churches of the preceding hundred years. The Friends churches fathered by George Fox were much closer than the Anglican churches from which they were excluded. The cultures of Friends churches were better than the others of those days. As people turn from non-Christian faith to Christ, some (like the Mizo churches of 1950) achieve a high degree of likeness to the divine model. Others bring in so many beliefs and practices of their pre-Christian faith that they must be judged to have achieved the divine model very imperfectly.

Empirical churches, though they are approximations of God's perfect revealed will, are

superior to all man-made models. I think it is
Thomas Aquinas who declares that the most
ignorant Christian has a better grasp of God's
truth than the wisest non-Christian. The most
imperfect church is closer to God's unchanging
truth than the best non-Christian society.

In vast Planet Earth, with its myriad segments
of society, its thousands of separate languages,
cultures, economic levels, and educational achieve-
ments, God's revelation, by his express order, is
not to be imposed on anyone. It is to be proclaimed. His ambassadors are to beseech men
to be reconciled to God according to his one
plan of salvation. They are to beseech, not to
force. They are to leave men and women free to
follow their own decisions. Otherwise acceptance
of Jesus Christ as the Savior and God as the
Father Almighty, becomes not acceptance by free
persons, but the mechanical action of puppets.

While Christians are thus, by divine command
and the example of Christ himself, to proceed on
the basis of religious freedom, they are to reject,
as they would Satan himself, the slick lie that all
opinions about absolute values, about God and
man, freedom and justice, eternal life and eternal
death, repentance and morality are equally true
and equally false. To this poisonous miasma,
God's Word returns an unequivocal *no*. God's
Word teaches that he has revealed the Truth and
this Truth will make men free.

There are indeed many speculations about
God. There *is* a wisdom of this world. God has
given men the ability to think and expects them
to do so. Man has been made in the image of
God and commanded to love God with all his
mind. Reason is a God-given ability and
Christians are reasonable persons. But God
directs us to test the spirits, to see the difference

between light and darkness, and to walk in the light. He says, discern evil paths and stay out of them. It is Satan who goes up and down the land teaching people that all religions are about equally true. The Bible does not counsel Christians to stash their thinking ability on the shelf and believe (quite against all evidence) that all life styles deliver an equal amount of the good life and are equally pleasing to God, all cultures are equally good, all ways lead to God, and all people will ultimately be saved.

On the contrary, from Genesis to Revelation, God's Word tells of one God, the Father Almighty, Maker of heaven and earth, who created the world, and then across thousands of years revealed his holy will to his people in myriad ways. The Bible is the inspired, authoritative, infallible rule of faith and practice. It is God's Word written. It proclaims that there is general revelation, which God gives to men as he desires in every age and every culture. God has also given special revelation in Jesus Christ his Son, our Savior, and in the Bible. All general revelation, inevitably mixed with the erroneous ideas of mere men, must be weighed and measured before special revelation. Everything not in accord with special revelation is either only partially true or completely false.

Is it intolerant to affirm this? We ask the question in the face of widespread contemporary feeling that there is no such thing as absolute truth, and therefore the position we have been advocating is an insult to the scientific outlook on life, is intolerant and unfriendly. We disagree. Various men do indeed hold differing convictions on eternal issues. Sometimes these arise on the grounds of what founders of the great religions have taught, sometimes on the "absolute truth" ardently proclaimed by some, namely that there is no absolute truth, and quite often on a person's desire for power or pleasure. It is not intolerant of such non-Christians to believe their convictions, or of Christians to believe that in Christ and the Bible God has revealed final truth concerning the eternal issues. The only intolerant man is the one who not only believes he is absolutely right, but forbids others to hold to their—to him erroneous—beliefs. He forces others to believe as he does.

Christians, on the contrary, hold that God has given men minds and expects them to use them. God did this, knowing that men would make mistakes. He gave them the right to disagree. He expects them to cleave to what *they* think is right. God expects Christians to do their best *to persuade all people* of the objective validity of God's revelation in the Bible and in Jesus Christ. Man's response to God in faith must be free. Every manner of coercion on the part of men concerning eternal issues should be excluded. If this is done, then ardency of belief is in no sense intolerant.

Christians portrayed in the New Testament were not intolerant. Peter was not intolerant when he announced "no other name." Our Lord was not intolerant when he said, "No one comes to the Father but by me." The early church never forced anyone to believe; though they did most ardently persuade them. It would be a sorry world if those who believe in what they consider good ways were to be prohibited from trying to persuade others to adopt them. All teaching of science, all sale of new inventions and technological improvements, and all advocacy of human rights would be prohibited. Any such demonstra-

tion of intolerance would advance the cause
neither of tolerance nor of human happiness.

Into this pluralistic world came God's Word
and God's Son, bearing authentic information
about who man is and who God is, about man's
duty and God's holy will, about God's plan of
salvation and his one way of life. God has not
left us to grope in a relativistic world. He has
shown us plainly what he requires of us.
Christians of many different cultural backgrounds,
languages, and degrees of technological knowledge
have studied God's Word and come up with
substantially similar understandings of the Way.

If the branches of the church, with all their
minor differences, are put on a single line of
distribution, and on this same line are located
Marxists, Hindus, Confucianists, Animists, Secularists, and Humanists, it will be seen that all
branches are grouped closely together. Away
from them by considerable distances are seen the
other life styles devised by men. If the Christian
denominations are now examined strictly by the
Word, it will be found that the closer they
adhere to the Word, the more rigorously they
exclude man-made doctrines which cannot be
substantiated from the mainstream of biblical
revelation, the more closely are they grouped
together. This happens completely independent of
the languages they speak and the cultures from
which they come. Devout Bible-reading and
Bible-obeying Christians from the islands of the
South Pacific, who 150 years ago were totally
illiterate cannibals, will be seen to be—in the
essentials of faith—remarkably like earnest Christians in Scotland who 150 years ago were totally
literate members of Christian churches. In short,
when God's revelation is accepted as the one

authority, the unchanging Word of God, then human opinions yield and a Christian way of life results.

In this Christian way of life, the good things in the Scotch and the Fijian cultures have been preserved. Indeed, they have been enhanced and made still more beautiful. All this has been achieved not by watering down biblical truth to fit ways of thinking about God and man which characterize other cultures, but rather by purging the wealth of the nations of all sin, sorrow, sickness, and death, and bringing it gleaming into Zion. It glows more brightly. It shines more steadily. The whole Church is richer because of the enriched contributions of many cultures.

This volume, being written in the midst of a pluralistic society suffering from an epidemic of relativism, maintains that according to the Scriptures there is only one Way, one Name, and one Savior. God's command stands firm: "Thou shalt have no other gods." It is really remarkable how very exclusive the Scriptures are. When the Bible is examined from the point of view of whether it allows for many different ways of life, all about equally true and equally false, there is no question as to the outcome of the investigation. The Bible does not know of many different mediators; there is only one. The Bible does not know of many different ways; there is only one. Early Christians were known as fol-lowers of *the* Way (Acts 9:2). Eternal life is not available to any except those who "have the Son." Only those who believe in Jesus Christ "will never die."

The proper Christian response to pluralistic society is not a question as to whether Christians are possessed by absolute truth or possess it. The proper response is firmly but intelligently to affirm that God in his revelation, the Bible, has shown the way, while granting cheerfully that other ways have much that is true and good in them. Indeed, many Christians hold that all truth, all goodness anywhere, is rooted in God's general revelation, but that no human system is therefore equal to his special revelation in the Bible and in Christ. It stands supreme. To be sure, more light will break from the Bible, but it will be light in harmony with what God in Christ has already revealed. New light will never contradict that. So Christians, as long as they depend on the Bible, may be certain as to the truth of what they believe, the standards they follow, and the ultimate Rock to which they anchor their lives. Believing this, they proclaim the one Way with power and gentle persuasiveness.

A word is in order as to how the book came to be written. Dr. Winfield Arn led a party to the Holy Land, and after that to Greece, Constantinople, and Rome. He invited me to go along and speak to members of the party in the various places visited on how the church grew there. I found this a fascinating adventure. It forced me to go back to the Scriptures which were written in those lands, under those skies, by men who had walked across those hills and sailed those seas. Being on a possible site of the Crucifixion and living in imagination those terrible hours, which the Bible tells us were spent "according to the definite plan and foreknowledge of God," was a transforming experience. Rolling across the hills over which the refugee Christians fled on foot to escape the persecution launched by Saul, I was amazed that *refugees* had spread the gospel enormously. From place to place the pilgrimage gave opportunity to think how the early church had grown, and what universal principles were to be discerned from the biblical record of that spread throughout the ancient world. These would be important for church growth in the contemporary world.

Dr. Arn and I found ourselves discovering in a new way the exclusiveness of Christ's claim. We had known something of this. No one can read the Bible without running across some of these emphases, but we were unprepared for the way in which hundreds of passages (in book after book, in Old Testament and New Testament, by writer after writer) reinforced the message that God's one plan of salvation, formed at the beginning of time and developed across centuries of biblical history, had culminated in Jesus Christ our Lord. All portrayed a single Way, a single Name, a single plan of salvation, a Savior seated on a solitary throne. He is the sole fountain of eternal life. He is the only Mediator between God and man.

This, we became convinced, had special meaning for our pluralistic society. However, if we are to understand it and the full meaning of the biblical revelation, we must see that the ancient world, in which God chose to give that revelation, was every bit as pluralistic as ours. The great religions of Greece and Rome, Egypt and Persia, India and China were greatly influential. Christianity was tiny and totally unknown. It would have been much easier for Jesus of Nazareth and the apostles to say, "What we proclaim is true for us Jews. Something else may be true for you." But instead, the Lord Jesus proclaimed the Kingdom of God—one God and one King. In Athens Paul declared, "Since we are God's offspring, we ought not to imagine that His nature resembles gold or silver or marble or anything sculptured by the art and imaginative faculty of man. Those times of ignorance (when men made such gods) God overlooked; but now commands all men everywhere to repent and believe on Jesus Christ."

Early Christians had every human reason to consider other ways at least as true as theirs. To shout aloud that the one Savior was a crucified Jew was a logical impossibility. Yet that is exactly what they did. They went everywhere preaching the gospel. If we think it difficult for us today to counter the tides of relativism, we should remember that it was ten times more difficult for the Christians in the first century to do so. But they disregarded the tides and proclaimed the Word with boldness. They were certain. They believed intensely. Unshakable conviction was one of the secrets of church growth in the early church.

It is still a main secret of growth today. Church growth rises from theological roots, from Christian certainty. People of unshakable conviction can profitably employ many insights from the social sciences and from communication and management, but without certainty all human resources suddenly become mere methods. Without certainty all the swords of the church suddenly become wooden. The absolute certainty of the early church (so well proclaimed by Scripture, probably for just such an age as this, in which relativism is enshrined in the contemporary ethos) must be recaptured if the church is to be healthy and to fulfill its God-given function.

Dr. Arn and I, remembering our journey through Bible lands, trust that readers will find interesting the frequent references to Jerusalem, Athens, Thessalonica, Galilee, Rome, and Corinth. The concepts set forth in this book did arise on that journey. This study of God's Word did begin under those skies. This welding of church growth today to church growth in the dawn of Christian expansion has led to fresh insights.

We also trust that readers themselves will examine the Scriptures in the light of today, in the midst of this pluralistic confusion which asserts so loudly, "God has not spoken. Each man and each culture is the final authority. Right is what 51 percent of the people vote for. If it feels good, do it. Let everyone do his own thing." To us, that dogma is foolish and utterly opposed to God's Word. But, readers, examine the Scriptures yourselves. We hope your investigation leads you to a new discovery of how germanely the Bible speaks to our contemporary world— this pluralistic society. You are studying the Lordship of Christ in a pluralistic world.

Donald A. McGavran

I
One Way

The early church grew explosively. The number of the disciples multiplied greatly. A great many of the priests were obedient to the faith. Multitudes became new creatures in Christ and were indwelt by the Holy Spirit.

But what sparked this mighty surge of church growth?

The growth of the church is seldom the result of just one factor; however, the fantastic growth of the early church was powerfully influenced by one unshakable conviction: that belief in Jesus Christ was essential for salvation. In Christ alone do people have new life as a gift from God. In him alone is forgiveness of sins, and joy and peace. Righteousness comes only by his grace and not by men's good actions. The early Christians were also certain that without Christ people were really lost.

Where did this revolutionary truth come from?

It came from Jesus Christ himself! He taught it fervently on every occasion. For three long years the Lord steadily saturated the minds of his disciples with the truth that to believe in him was to pass from death to life. Faith in Christ was the pearl of great price, and to obtain that pearl, one must sell all that he has. Day after day, month after month, in town after town, in varying circumstances Jesus Christ deliberately planted this truth in the minds of his disciples. His teachings concerning the lost and the way of salvation were given again and again, in particular places to particular persons. The details are important, for they anchor the incidents to reality.

What a joy to travel the very roads the Lord

traveled and to see the limestone-capped hills he
saw. The narrow grain fields between the hills
must be very like those he walked through. The
summer is a dry, brown season, but in the
spring, rains make Palestine a green and pleasant
land. In these surroundings, among these very
hills, throughout his three-year ministry, the
Lord continually announced and emphasized the
fact that belief in him was essential for salvation.

Today we hear so much teaching on the
kindness and love of Christ that some are
surprised at his uncompromising insistence that
the one road to salvation is narrow. The salvation
is positive and glorious, but there is only one
road to it. Unless a person believes on the One
whom the Father has sent, he is without true life.
On the day of Judgment, Christ taught, he will
disown all who, not believing in him, have failed
to turn from darkness to light. All the Gospels
speak clearly to this point. Whatever else the
Lord Jesus taught, he certainly taught this: that
he alone is the way to salvation and eternal life.

This teaching saturates the inspired record. The
Gospels all announce that he is the way to
abundant, eternal life and that without belief in
him, men are really lost. His disciples, who lived
with him constantly, had this truth burned into
their consciousness and inscribed on their hearts.
This conviction controlled their actions in the
wonderful years following Pentecost and was one
of the principal causes of church growth.

As we sat in the ruins of Capernaum on the
floor of the ancient church which began in the
fishermen's quarter where Simon Peter probably
lived, we remember the words of Christ, "I am
the way. No one comes to the Father but by me."

The truth that he is *the* one way is particularly
clear in his answer to a question recorded in John

6:28: "What must we do, to be doing the work of God?" He might have answered in many ways. He might have said, "Repent of your sins." He might have said, "Do justice, love kindness, and walk humbly with your God." He might have said, "Fear God." He said none of these. Jesus answered, "This is the work of God, that you believe in him whom God has sent."

Another incident emphasized the truth that without Christ men are really lost. Jesus began to teach the people about John the Baptist. He said, "Among those born of women there has risen no one greater than John the Baptist" (Matt. 11:11). Not Moses, not Elisha, not David, not Solomon, not Alexander the Great, not Plato, not Socrates, not Augustus Caesar. No one born of a woman is greater than John the Baptist. Our Lord continued, "He who is least in the kingdom of heaven is greater than he." The kingdom of heaven is composed of those who obey the King. Jesus Christ is the risen and reigning King. He is the Head of the Church. He is to be obeyed. The truly great ones are those who are in the kingdom of heaven, and the least in that kingdom, though he be illiterate or destitute, is greater than the richest and wisest outside it. How essential it is that we obey the King and be part of the Kingdom of God!

Caesarea Philippi was both a city and a district in the upper reaches of the Jordan River north of the Sea of Galilee. The district was one through which Jesus and his disciples often traveled. It was probably in these villages of North Galilee that the Lord first sent out the twelve. In his instructions to them he said, "Everyone who hears the gospel from you and then acknowledges me before men, I also will acknowledge before my Father who is in heaven, but whoever denies me before men I will also deny before my Father who is in heaven." The familiarity of the passage must not hide from us the terrible seriousness of the words. What men and women do concerning Jesus Christ determines their eternal destiny. That is the clear meaning of his teaching.

There will be a judgment. All will give account for what they do with the person of Jesus Christ. Those who deny him, he will deny. Those who confess him, he will confess before his Father. The one thing that will count at that judgment is knowing Christ and having confessed him.

In these same villages he made another dramatic and drastic statement: "He who loves father or mother more than me is not worthy of me." It is not enough to pay tribute to him in some vague way, belong to his church, champion the poor, or do good. To be a worthy follower of Christ, the disciple must love him much more than he loves father and mother, wife or husband, son or daughter. Christ must be first!

Jesus taught that unless men and women believe in him, they are really lost. Such passages occur again and again in the New Testament. This truth was never questioned by the early church.

In sending out the twelve, Jesus said, "If anyone will not receive you, shake off the dust from your feet" (Matt. 10:14). Now listen to the terrible words which followed: "Truly it shall be more tolerable on the day of judgment for the land of Sodom and Gomorrah than for that town." Christ sent them out to announce that the kingdom of heaven was at hand. He sent them out to announce that the King had come. If the listeners did not yield allegiance to the King,

judgment awaited—judgment worse than that
meted out to those fearfully wicked cities of
Sodom and Gomorrah.

In Mark 8:34-38 the truth is reiterated. The
Lord Jesus taught his disciples:

*If any man would come after me, let him deny
himself, take up the cross and follow me. For whoever
would save his life will lose it; and whoever loses his
life for my sake and the gospel will save it. For what
does it profit a man, to gain the whole world and
forfeit his life? For what can a man give in return for
his life? For whoever is ashamed of me and my words
in this adulterous and sinful generation, of him will
the Son of Man also be ashamed when he comes in
the glory of his father with the holy angels.*

Do we hear what he is saying? The supreme
event will happen when the Lord comes in all his
glory. Compared with being received *then* by the
King, saving one's life, comfort, fame, wealth, and
power are of no importance whatever. They are
mere temporal conveniences—something entirely
different from eternal salvation.

Let us recall the rich young ruler. He came to
the Master when Jesus, coming south from
Galilee, was in Judea beyond the Jordan. The
rulers in Judea were the Sadducees, the aris-
tocracy of the time. The rich young ruler was
a well bred, wealthy young man. He asked,
"Good Teacher, what must I do to inherit eternal
life?" (Luke 18:18). Our Lord answered, "You
know the commands." The young man quickly
replied, "All these have I kept from my youth."
Then Jesus said to him, "One thing you still lack.
Sell all that you have and distribute to the poor
and you will have treasure in heaven; *and come,
follow me."*

But for the last four words, one might
understand the Lord to mean that salvation
comes by works. You are saved by obeying the
law, and by selling your goods and distributing
the money to the poor, by philanthropy and
goods works. But in view of the last four words
and the other passages we have been recalling,
this passage must be interpreted as follows: "You
believe in me a little, but your basic allegiance is
to your great wealth. You cannot serve two
masters. If you would inherit eternal life you
must renounce your allegiance to your wealth.
Sell all you have. Burn your bridges to the
security of this world. *Come follow me.* You
cannot enter the kingdom of heaven unless you
value me above every earthly treasure."

In the parable of the Great Banquet, our
Lord's teaching is so clear. A man gave a great
banquet. The prosperous, the prestigious, the
leaders, the eminent citizens—all were invited.
But when the banquet was ready, the guests
began to make excuses, and no one came. The
man giving the feast turned to his servants and
said, "Go out into the highways and byways and
compel the people to come." Then he added this:
"None of these men who were invited shall taste
my banquet." The great, the rich, the educated,
the men of good character, *if they do not come to
my banquet shall not taste it at all.* Without Christ
is anyone saved? The testimony of the Scriptures
is clear. Christ is the Way—the only Way to
abundant eternal life. Christ's own words declare
again and again that people will not even taste
true life unless they believe on him.

Still another illustration is recorded in the fifth
chapter of John. Jesus, speaking to his disciples,
says, "He that hears my words and believes on
him who sent me has eternal life—he has passed

from death to life." Who passes from death to life? A just man? No. A brave man? No. An intelligent man? No. He who hears my word and believes on him who sent me, *he* will have eternal life. Belief in Christ is the only bridge from death to life.

So intense was this belief held by early Christians that they were willing to die for it. As we walked through the catacombs of Rome, the underground cemeteries in which, during persecutions, the early church used to meet, we saw the graphic evidence of the unshakable conviction of those Christians. They staked their lives on the truth that the one essential thing was belief in Jesus Christ, Savior and Lord. Men and women were better off to die believing in Christ than to live in comfort denying him. Christians then numbered only those who believed with all their hearts that without Christ people were really lost, but that with him, death itself was gain. When Christians were threatened with being thrown to the lions in the Colosseum, they could easily have saved themselves by denying Christ and offering a pinch of incense to Caesar. Why didn't they? Because they believed the Lord Jesus who said that it is better to enter the Kingdom of God with one eye than with two to be thrown into hell. He would soon welcome them to eternal blessedness.

The overpowering conviction of this "one way" came from the teaching of the Lord Jesus Christ. That was its origin, its fountainhead, its first source. It had a second source, the teaching of the apostles. In the earliest days of the church, the apostles declared that faith in Jesus Christ was essential for salvation. For example, Peter, standing in the portico of Solomon's temple (Acts 3:11), spoke forth-

rightly about Jesus as being *the* Messiah, the
One foretold by Moses and the prophets, the
one seed of Abraham in whom all the families
of the earth were to be blessed. There was no
other. Men and women either acknowledged
him as "both Lord and Messiah" or were
counted among those who did "not heed."
Concerning these latter, Peter declared, "Every
soul that does not heed that prophet shall be
utterly destroyed from among the people"
(3:23).

The best known passage carrying this
unequivocal announcement is, of course, Acts
4:12: "There is salvation in no one else; for
there is no other name under heaven, that has
been given among men, by which we must be
saved."

It is important to realize that this passage
sums up what the Lord himself repeatedly said,
what the apostles proclaimed, and what the
early church believed was unshakable fact. The
gospel always assumed the truth voiced in the
many passages quoted here.

Paul also, from the beginning to the end of
his ministry, proclaimed a Savior whom it is
necessary to believe. As he said to the
philosophers on Mars Hill: "God is now
declaring to men that all everywhere should
repent because He has fixed a day in which He
will judge the world . . . through a Man whom
he has appointed" (Acts 17:30, 31 NASB).

God had overlooked the days of ignorance,
but now it was repent and believe on Christ—
or come under the judgment of God.

No worldly advantage counts when weighed
against the blessedness of being in Christ. In
Philippians 3:8, Paul writes that he counts all
his worldly treasures—splendid education, posi-

tion, wealth, honor—as loss in order to gain Christ and be found in him. Not only did Paul say these words, but his whole life demonstrated this scale of values.

In 2 Corinthians 11:23 Paul recounts what he has suffered as a faithful servant of the gospel: scourgings, shipwrecks, imprisonments, and on and on—an impressive list. Paul had been commissioned, he tells us in Romans 1:5, to bring about obedience of faith among the Gentiles. He suffered gladly in carrying out his commission to bring Gentiles to Christ. He was absolutely confident that all those outside of Christ, be they Jew or Gentile, were without true life. God wanted them to hear the gospel of salvation and to accept it, to walk in the light, to know the power of God. Modern secularists may doubt that man without Christ is lost, but the scholar Paul was certain of it.

Paul never knew Christ in the flesh. In view of Galatians 1:12, some are inclined to think that Paul's convictions concerning his Master were arrived at independently of Jesus' teaching and that of the apostles. However, that is not what he himself says. This passage declares that his gospel—that Gentiles could be saved by faith in Jesus Christ—was given him by special revelation. We must not stretch that truth and make it mean that he had heard nothing of the essential teaching and of the life, death, and resurrection of the Lord. Indeed, without those teachings, his gospel would have been inconceivable.

Observe the many occasions on which this man, so extraordinarily quick to learn, could have and must have learned of our Lord's teaching that belief in him was necessary for salvation. For instance, during Saul's years in Jerusalem, when he was persecuting the church, he certainly heard that teaching of Jesus again and again from people betting their lives that it was true. That teaching burned its way into Saul's memory.

After the Lord appeared to him on the Damascus Road, Saul was instructed for days, weeks, and perhaps months, by Ananias and other disciples. Saul visited Peter for a few weeks and listened to him intently. Paul was an intimate of Barnabas who knew the Lord's teaching very well. In the light of all these contacts, we conclude that Paul knew Jesus' teaching that "no one comes to the Father but by me." He constantly declared it in many ways.

All the epistles are missionary documents, written by missionaries to young churches and young Christians. Again and again the epistles testify to the fact that belief in Christ is necessary for salvation. Nothing else brings a man from darkness to light and from death to life. Nothing else confers on him the glorious inheritance of full, free, eternal life. The New Testament is God's revelation of his concern for lost mankind—a concern proclaimed by Christ, by the apostles, and by the early church. That church spread through the Roman Empire on the basic conviction that whether close relatives or citizens of a far-off land, people outside of Christ are lost—and God wants them found. He has prepared for them one Way of salvation.

We are often tempted to believe that missionary activity of the church depended solely on the Great Commission, but the Great Commission really is the capstone on the teachings the Lord Jesus had given day after day, week after week, and month after month, throughout his ministry. That teaching was that it was absolutely necessary to believe on him whom the Father has sent.

True life here and hereafter became available when people recognized this . . . when they followed him . . . when they sold all they had for the pearl of great price . . . when they acknowledged Jesus Christ as the King and thus entered the Kingdom of God. This was the supremely important act. The Great Commission is simply Christ's summary of all these teachings. Even had the Great Commission not been given, the apostles with these truths blazing brightly in their souls, could scarcely have done anything else than to seek the lost and bring them from animal life to the glorious life of children of God. That is what their Lord had come to do: to seek and save the lost. That is what he commanded them to do.

How does all this relate to the growth of the church today? For one thing, we must take the passages mentioned, and numerous others in the Gospels and the epistles, much more seriously. *Lasting church growth requires convictional support.* Church growth is not merely good methods, better management, and multiplying Class Two workers. Church growth is not merely recognizing homogeneous units. Churches grow not merely because they evangelize receptive individuals and deliberately become friendly churches. To be sure, these good things will help. A spurt of growth will likely take place. But without Bible-based conviction, churches will become religious clubs and lapse back into a stagnant condition. Christians must have unshakable conviction that belief on Christ is essential to becoming new creatures, essential to salvation, essential to the achievement of a just social order, essential for eternal life. Without Christ, people are really in the dark; with him they walk confidently in the light.

Theologians will recognize that we have been voicing Christological convictions. Theologians say that Jesus Christ is ontologically one with the Father. By this they affirm in philosophical language what the first three verses of John's Gospel say in plain English. Colossians 2 declares that in Christ "dwells *the whole fullness of* deity bodily." Jesus Christ is one with the Father. He is co-equal with the Father in purpose and action. "He who has seen me has seen the Father." This biblical teaching is not an easy doctrine. Scientific naturalism, which excludes God from a mechanically conceived universe, finds it impossible to believe in the Christ of the Bible. Those who live in an intellectual atmosphere heavily impregnated with scientific naturalism find it difficult to believe either in a personal God or that Jesus Christ is one with the Father.[1] Yet this is what the Bible affirms without hesitation. Matthew and Hebrews, John and Paul, Luke and Mark, all set forth this teaching clearly. Scripture teaches both our Lord's full humanity and his full deity. The "one way" of which we write is the way which God the Father Almighty, Maker of heaven and earth, in an entirely supernatural way, according to his own pleasure deliberately revealed. Others may explain it away in various ingenious ways, but biblical Christians simply believe what the Bible teaches. Jesus Christ is the way, the truth, and the life. No one comes to the Father but by him.

Anthropologists and missionaries trained in that discipline will recognize that in this first chapter we have been speaking to a burning

---

[1]Science itself, of course, says nothing on the point. While science is very useful in things which can be weighed and measured, it cannot deal with all dimensions of reality.

question in modern missions—to what extent
may Christianity adapt itself to the various
cultures in which it multiplies believers and
churches? Is there one way, or are there many
ways?

Certainly there will be some adaptation.
The new believers who speak Hindi will read
their Bibles and think and pray in Hindi. They
become Christians in their Hindi culture.
Congregations with an average income of $200 a
year per household will not worship God or
celebrate the communion in the same way as
those in which households have an average
income of $30,000 a year. But what are the
limits of adaptation? When does adaptation
become betrayal of the Christian faith and the
biblical revelation? *The Clash of Christianity with
Cultures* by Donald McGavran is an extended
discussion of the problem, but here a brief quota-
tion from his 1972 book *Crucial Issues in Missions
Tomorrow* will suffice. It will show that the Christian faith respects cultures without in the least
compromising the one Way which is Jesus Christ.
It is essential in propagating the Christian faith,
he says,

*to respect cultures, to affirm that they contain much
that is good and must be preserved, and to deny that
"the advance of Christianity is over the dead cultures
it conquers." Equally truly, it is essential to remember
that Christ is the only begotten Son of God, the Word
who was in the beginning with the Father, through
whom everything was made, and before whom all men
and all cultures will be judged. The everlasting God
has chosen to give His revelation to men in the Bible
which passes from culture to culture, purging each of
them repeatedly as new light breaks from it. It purges
all cultures—Christian, partially Christian and non-*

Christian alike. Since it purges twentieth-century
Christianity in a way it did not purge seventeenth-
century Christianity, it also purges twentieth-century
Bantu religion and Marxist religion as their adherents
come to believe on Jesus Christ (pp. 25-26).

If a congregation holds a sub-Christian position
concerning the lostness of mankind, how can we
remedy the situation? If it doubts whether anyone
is ever really lost, if it has read more of Aldous
Huxley and *Time* magazine than of John the
Evangelist, a good starting place is to teach what
the Lord actually said. The few passages of
Scripture in this chapter are a small sample.
Many others also should be studied.

The Lord repeatedly burned this tremendous
revelation into the minds of his followers. The
disciples did not believe it easily. They did not
come to Jesus believing in him as the Messiah—
the only Messiah. But after three years with him,
they did believe. In any congregation, if the
people are fed on the Word, they come to
believe the Word. Part of the problem in
churches today is weak Bible preaching. If we
communicate what the Scriptures clearly say and
what the Lord beyond question said, then the
same convictions which gradually formed in the
minds of the disciples will be born and grow in
today's Christians. Once that happens, the good
methods we use will bear more fruit and more
lasting fruit.

2
No
Other
Name

*I*n Jerusalem the great multitude which gathered on the day of Pentecost did not know what was happening. They watched in high excitement, wondering what God would do next. A tremendous reversal of expectations had occurred. The Sanhedrin and the Romans had, beyond doubt, killed Jesus of Nazareth. He was finished. But then rumor, circulating wildly, suggested that he had risen from the grave. And here before their very eyes a mysterious outpouring of power on ordinary people was going on. Jewish pilgrims from many parts of the Roman world heard in the languages and dialects of Mesopotamia, Pontus, Egypt, and other provinces (Acts. 2:8, 11, 37) what these Galileans were saying. They heard Peter, a fisherman from Galilee, proclaiming with absolute certainty, "Let the whole House of Israel know beyond all doubt that God has made Him both Lord and Messiah—this Jesus whom you crucified" (Acts 2:36 Moffatt).

The impossible was happening. The common people—many of whom had been his followers— were filled with unspeakable joy. The true and living God, they were now sure, had revealed himself in the person of Jesus of Nazareth. Beyond all doubt, God *had* made him both Lord and Messiah. The passages from Joel and the Psalms, which Peter quoted so convincingly, certainly fit Jesus, his crucifixion and resurrection, and the outpouring of the Holy Spirit which was going on before their eyes. How could they doubt? Conviction solidified that what God had foretold by the mouths of his prophets hundreds of years before had in very truth come to pass. Jesus, "a man sent from God and accredited as

such by miracles and marvels and signs which
God did through him" had risen from the dead.
The resurrection proved that he was truly the
Messiah—the only Messiah.

The resurrection had occurred fifty days ago
and was being proclaimed only now, fifty days
later. We must therefore ask, how had these
Galileans come to make this astounding announcement with such absolute certainty?

This conviction, born in their minds as the
risen Lord had repeatedly shown himself to them,
had been maturing in the hundred and twenty for
fifty days. The new understanding of the Messiah
was taking shape. The meaning of the life, death,
and resurrection of Jesus became clearer and
clearer.

It was not merely that God had raised Jesus
from the dead. This stupendous event gained
tremendous meaning from what the risen Lord
had explained to "the eleven and the rest" in
Jerusalem, namely, that "everything written . . .
in the Law of Moses and in the prophets and in
the psalms concerning me must be fulfilled"
(Luke 24.44-47). The resulting radically new
understanding of the nature and function of the
Messiah took weeks to mature. No doubt the
passages from scrolls of Scripture were read and
their revolutionary meaning was gradually recognized. Instead of the earthly Messiah, a greater
Judas Maccabeus—which is what they all
expected—the Messiah intended by God was
quite different. He "was pierced through for our
transgressions." By "his scourging we are healed"
(Is. 53:5 NASB). The crucifixion had taken place,
not as a defeat of God's plans, but *according to
the definite plan and foreknowledge of God.*" A new
and glorious life was made possible to all who
believed on Jesus Messiah and became his

disciples. As the fifty days passed, the hundred and twenty gained more and more new understandings of the authentic Messiah—Savior, King, Comforter, Guide, Giver of Eternal Life and Inner Joy, Bestower of the peace which passes understanding. The little band of a hundred and twenty believers rejoiced in all this, but *told no one*. They were still putting it all together. They were common people. They did not have courage. They were not public speakers. *They kept quiet.*

Then came Pentecost. They were all gathered in one place. The outpouring of the Holy Spirit on them all, in the house where they were sitting, drove them out to do what they had not done during the fifty days—tell others the glorious good news of the Messiah. When the hundred and twenty heard the mighty wind and saw a tongue as of fire resting on the head of each of them, a power entirely outside themselves filled them with joy and gave them the ability to speak in "other tongues." Weymouth translates the Greek for "other tongues" as "foreign languages."

Their conviction grew that the resurrection (of which they were quite certain) was God's final seal on the authentic Messiah foretold by Moses, psalmists, and prophets. Thus formed a reasoned and unwavering certainty that the life, death, resurrection, and presence of the Messiah had not just happened, but was the fixed and determined purpose of God. The God of Abraham, Isaac, and Jacob had caused it to happen. They stood in the beginning of the new age. The Christians were betting their lives that Jesus was the ultimate Power in the universe, seated at the right hand of God; that he had filled his followers with joy and forgiven their sins. God had in very truth made him both Lord and Messiah. A whole new way of life, a whole new understanding of sin and salvation—open to all who believed, including common people—had been lived out before them. That which they had heard, had seen with their own eyes, and had touched with their own hands, they could not doubt. The enormous import of the new understanding of Jesus of Nazareth filled their minds. *Everyone had to be told at once of this amazing event.*

Driven out by the Holy Spirit, bubbling over with the tremendous significance for all of the revolutionary new understanding of the nature and function of the Messiah, overjoyed at the realization that the crucifixion was not a shameful death (though the Sanhedrin intended it to be that) but the opening of eternal life to all who believed, they rushed out of the house to address the great crowd which, hearing "the sound from heaven," had gathered outside.

They started telling the great good news. Their conviction concerning the true understanding of the Messiah sustained the hundred and twenty when they stood before the multitude, *testifying to Jesus.* We do not know how many of the hundred and twenty were speaking, but, according to the record, it seems likely that all the eleven and probably many others were proclaiming the exciting news at the same time. God had in very truth raised Jesus from the dead and thus fulfilled the Old Testament prophecies. Jesus of Nazareth was alive, was the Messiah, was the ultimate Power in the universe, was seated at the right hand of God. He filled his followers with great joy. He granted them forgiveness of sins. They walked light. Everyone had to be told of this amazing event, this beginning of a new age, this good news of Jesus.

As they spoke, many voices together shouting the good news, men of many provinces (Parthians, Medes, Elamites, residents of Mesopotamia, Judea, Cappadocia, Pontus, Asia, Phrygia, Pamphilia, Egypt, the part of Libya belonging to Cyrene, and visitors from Rome, Cretans, and Arabians—the names pour forth without any order) miraculously heard, each in his own mother tongue, the many witnesses announcing to them "the mighty works of God."

Then at some appropriate pause in the tumult which resulted as the crowd listened to the many excited witnesses, Peter started speaking, evidently alone. All the rest of the witnesses apparently listened. He set forth in logical, historical fashion the common conviction of the Christians, ending with the tremendous affirmation, "Let all the house of Israel therefore assuredly know that God has made him both Lord and Christ, this Jesus whom you crucified" (2:36). The absolute certainty of the announcement is what we underscore.

A few days later, while Peter and John were proclaiming to the common people that God had raised Jesus from the dead and made him Messiah, "the priests, the Commander of the Temple Guard, and the Sadducees came upon them." Incensed at their seditious teaching, they arrested them and threw them into jail. The next day the two apostles were brought before the Sanhedrin, made to stand in the center, and asked, "By what power and in what name did you heal the lame man?" Peter's bold reply to that prestigious body, the ultimate authority in religious and cultural matters, culminates in this declaration: "There is salvation in no one else, for there is no other name under heaven given among men by which we must be saved" (Acts 4:12 RSV). The announcement is particularly

impressive because of the terrible, unforgivable
threat the priests and Sadducees had heard Peter
voicing the day before, and hearing which they
had arrested him. Quoting from Deuteronomy
18:15 and Leviticus 23:29, he had insisted:
"Everyone, without exception, who refuses to
listen to that prophet (Jesus) shall be *utterly
destroyed* from among the people" (Acts 3:23
Weymouth) (emphasis ours).

We should not take these passages of Scripture
merely as records of Peter's preaching. They were
that, to be sure, but in addition and more
important, they are records *of the unshakable
consensus of the early church.* This was the common
testimony of thousands of Christians.

On this flaming conviction, the early church
grew uncontrollably, irresistibly.

This same certainty burned in the heart of the
Apostle Paul. In writing to the Galatians he is
sure that Jesus Christ is Lord according to the
will of God the Father. He writes, ". . . peace
from God the Father, and our Lord Jesus Christ,
who gave himself for our sins *according to the will
of our God and Father*" (emphasis ours). Paul
shared the conviction of the entire early church.
The apostles had it—the ordinary people had it—
those who believed and were baptized on the day
of Pentecost had it. Paul, the persecutor of the
church, came to believe it as firmly as anyone
else. This conviction blazed so strongly in the
early Christians that they were willing to go to
prison, to be beaten publicly, and to give their
lives testifying that there was "no other Name"
but that of Jesus Christ, the Lord.

In the New Testament, Jesus is called "Lord"
hundreds of times. In the Gospels, the title was
often used without intending to assert that Jesus
was the only Lord. Weymouth translates the

Greek word as "Sir." Thus the woman taken in
adultery replies "No one, Sir," and the blind man
cured at the pool of Siloam on seeing Jesus
declared, "I believe, Sir." In Acts and the epistles,
however, the title "Lord" generally means "the
one and only Lord,"[1] the risen and reigning Lord,
the Lord who is to be worshiped, the Lord by
whose grace we live, the one Lord by belief in
whom salvation is to be gained, the Lord whose
grace the Christians invoke and for whose coming
they long. He is the King of kings and Lord of
lords. He knows who are his and is everywhere present. Everywhere he is Lord of all who
call on his Name. He is God's Son, Jesus,
Messiah—*and there is no other*. Paul writes "to all
those who call on the name of our Lord Jesus
Christ, both their Lord and ours" (1 Cor. 1:2
RSV).

It is beyond doubt that the early church
fervently believed that forgiveness of sins and
eternal life are available only through faith in
Jesus Christ. No one else has paid the price for
sin. No one else even claims to have done so.
There is no other Cross. No other way is known
to men whereby sin is maintained as sinful while
at the same time sinners are offered effective
forgiveness. John declares, "This is eternal life,
that they know thee, the only true God, and
Jesus Christ whom thou has sent." We also read,
"He who has the Son has life," and—more
definitively—"who has not the Son has not life."

These passages must not be seen as isolated
verses, or as the theology of certain writers and
not of others. Rather, they sum up what the early

---

[1] In the Septuagint, Lord, (*Kurios*) is commonly used for
Yahweh. This nuance probably is reflected in Acts and
the epistles.

church believed and taught. To be sure, it was not a systematized theology to which all alike subscribed—it was too early for that. Nor was it a pithy creed taught to all catechumens before baptism. Few at the time of baptism were acutely conscious of these certainties. The jailer at Philippi, baptized in the dead of night, probably had no clear concept of eternal life, let alone any certainty concerning it. Nevertheless, the teaching of the apostles and all responsible leaders of the church rose out of the white-hot experiences of the Crucifixion, Resurrection, and Pentecost. These were unique. There was, therefore, no other Savior, no other risen Lord, no other continuing Comforter, no other Name, no other Gospel. A striking unity of all the New Testament writers is apparent at this point. None of them proposes any other Savior, any other way of salvation. All are certain that the Name of Jesus is the only Name.

Paul declared that salvation comes not by works of righteousness but by grace through faith in the mighty Name of Jesus. Again and again Paul repeats this conviction. A man is not justified by works of the law, that is, by being just or doing justice, but through faith in Jesus Christ, the only Name, the powerful Name, the God-appointed way of salvation. Today we can be quite sure neither education, nor development, nor justice, nor restructured society, nor money, nor economic sytem, nor democratic government will save men. All these are good gifts of God. The church should work toward all of them but none has any salvific power. They will (sometimes) bring about temporal improvements, but eternal salvation is available only in the mighty Name of Jesus. The Church grew because it believed and acted upon this great truth.

The early church believed that not only was the Name of Jesus powerful, but it was also universal. This universal, powerful Name must be made known to all men everywhere. In writing to the Philippians, Paul says, "God has highly exalted Jesus and bestowed upon him the name which is above every name. That at the name of Jesus every knee should bow, in heaven and on earth and under the earth, and every tongue confess that Jesus Christ is Lord to the glory of God the Father." On this intensely missionary conviction the early church reached out, driven by compassion for people everywhere. All must be told of God's plan for men to be saved through faith in Jesus Christ.

Many in the scholarly community make entirely too much of the fact that in Paul's epistles there is not a single sentence urging Christians to go out and evangelize non-Christians. One eminent scholar (disregarding the many forms of the Great Commission and the many passages from the epistles to which I am calling attention) goes so far as to say, "There is absolutely nothing in the New Testament corresponding to the almost frantic appeals for missionary activity which have been common in Protestant missionary practice."

Quite the contrary, taking the message to the ends of the earth—according to numerous passages of the Bible—is an essential part of the will of God and hence the duty of Christians. In his epistle to Titus Paul writes that "the grace of God has appeared, bringing salvation to all men" (2:11). And to Timothy he writes, "The word of God is not imprisoned. For this reason I endure all things, for the sake of those (in every land of every tribe and kindred) who are chosen, that they may also obtain the salvation which is in

Christ Jesus and with it eternal glory" (2 Tim.
2:9, 10 NASB). In the Old Testament also God
has in numerous places revealed his unswerving
purpose that all tongues, tribes, and nations shall
hear the good news. For example Isaiah 42:6
reads,

I am the Lord. I have called you in righteousness.
I will also hold you by the hand and watch over you.
And I will appoint you as a covenant to the people,
As a light to the nations.

The shaky argument of those modern scholars
who play down the missionary mandate does,
however, gain a slight plausibility, because the
missionary activity of the last two centuries has
been carried on across huge physical, economic,
political, and linguistic gulfs. Ernest, not frantic,
appeals to this more difficult, less natural task
have been necessary. Missionaries have gone to
the other side of the world. They have journeyed
ten thousand miles. They have learned languages
totally other than their own. They have learned,
read, and written other scripts than their own.
They have gone from "have" to "have not"
nations. They have blazed completely new trails.
Mission activity in the New Testament was never
across such gulfs. Paul never went outside his
own culture medium. He spoke the Greek he had
learned as a boy in Tarsus. He was a Roman
citizen and—except for his few years in Rome—
evangelized *within 800 miles of his birthplace.* His
evangelization, and that to which he called the
saints, was therefore an exhortation to commend
the gospel by living as Christians in their own
social matrix. As Christians did this, they would
speak about Christ as naturally as Americans
would about a new car which got eighty miles to

the gallon of gas. They would, of course, tell their own kin and culture contacts of the wonderful new Source of power, peace, healing, and eternal life. Today we must appeal for the much more difficult cross-cultural evangelism.

As this book indicates, chapter after chapter, far from the New Testament's saying "absolutely nothing" about ardent evangelism, it is full of illustrations of it, demonstrations of it, and commands to do it. Peter writes that Christians are a chosen race, a royal priesthood. . . . "that you may declare the wonderful deeds of him who called you out of darkness into his marvelous light." Ephesians 3:10, 11 declares that it is the eternal purpose of God that through the church the manifold wisdom of God is to be made known to all principalities and powers and *all men* (emphasis ours). Philippians 2:14-16 tells us that Christians are to shine as lights in the dark world among crooked and perverse men to whom they proffer the Word of Life (Weymouth and NEB). Many other passages might be cited. According to the New Testament, evangelism is an essential characteristic of genuine Christians. They and the apostles are "partners in the gospel." They spread the good news as naturally as breathing.

We read of Paul's intense longing that his kinsmen believe on Christ and be saved (Romans 10:1 and 9:1-3). We recall Romans 16:25, which I call the Great Commission according to Paul, where the inspired writer asserts that the very gospel itself, by Eternal God's command, has been revealed to win *panta ta ethne*, "to obedience to the faith" (Weymouth). The New Testament from beginning to end throbs with conviction that Christians ought to tell others of the only Name. When we ponder Paul's enduring

passion to win Gentiles to eternal life and read
his repeated messages to his converts that he had
been a father to them and they, as good sons and
daughters, ought to do as he had done, it is
impossible for us to hold that Paul could have
regarded with favor Christians unconcerned with
the salvation of neighbors and relatives.

In 2 Corinthians, Paul declares that as grace
extends to more and more people (through faith
in Jesus Christ), thanksgiving to the glory of God
increases. It can scarcely be doubted that Paul
accepted his commission, received on the
Damascus Road and in Damascus, because he
recognized it as his part of the church's task to
preach the gospel to the whole creation and to
disciple all the tribes and families of earth. If the
church had not been sent into the world to lead
it to believe on Christ, it would have made little
sense for Paul to carry the gospel to the Gentiles.
Paul's consciousness of his commission was a key
element in his entire ministry. He refers to it
again and again. He received his marching orders
very early in the Christian era—possibly as early
as A.D. 31. He saw them as a subhead under the
great command to spread the gospel to Jerusalem,
Judea, Samaria, *and the ends of the earth.*

Belief in the Name which is above every name
was no invention of Peter, Paul, or the early
Christians. God himself had revealed his own
personal name. As recorded in the Old
Testament, God spoke to Moses in the burning
bush, and told him to bring the sons of Israel out
of Egypt. Moses said to God, "The sons of Israel
may say to me, 'What is His name?' What shall
I say to them?" And God said to Moses, "I AM
WHO I AM. . . . you shall say to the sons of
Israel, 'I AM has sent me to you' (Exodus 3:2-14
NASB). It is certainly more than coincidence that

Jesus of Nazareth again and again said "I am." I am the way. I am the truth. I am the life. No one comes to the Father but by me. I am the light of the world. I am the bread of life. Before Abraham was, I am. This mysterious name, by which God has revealed himself, was used again and again by Jesus. I Am, Lord, Savior, Shepherd, Teacher, Son of God, Lord of lords, Giver of Eternal Life. His is the only Name by which men can be saved. No wonder the early church grew. It believed this truth as an incontestable fact of life.

Human beings have no native ability to discern God's nature and God's will. They are creatures. He is the Creator. My ways are not your ways, says the Lord. But God has graciously revealed himself to us. The Bible says, "All that may be known of God lies plain before men's eyes; indeed God himself has disclosed it to them" (Romans 1:19, 20 NEB). "Things beyond our seeing, things beyond our hearing, things beyond our imagining—these it is that God has revealed to us through his Spirit" (1 Cor. 2:9, 10 NEB). "The world did not know God through wisdom" but through revelation which seemed folly to the philosophers of the world (1 Cor. 1:21 ASV).

To be sure, in all ages men have speculated about God, but their speculations are a curious combination of truth and falsehood, of the sublime and the ridiculous, of the pure and the base. Men have made images of God—dogs, cats, snakes, turtles, men, women, phallic emblems, money—but apart from God's self-disclosure and affirmation about himself, all else is guess work, some of it rather good. The only confident basis for knowledge about God, the only way to estimate what in general revelation is from God, is what it has pleased him to reveal to us through his Word and his Son.

The early church did *not* include those who contemptuously disbelieved that Jesus Christ is the Son of God—the power of God—the only Name by which men can be saved. Part of our impotence today arises from the fact that in our congregations and denominations are some of that kind of people.

Visitors to Corinth can stand on the very spot where Gallio the proconsul held court and where the Jews brought Paul before him, charging that Paul was "persuading men to worship God contrary to the law" (Acts 18:13 RSV). What had Paul been saying? He had been preaching the only way of salvation: Christ crucified (1 Cor. 2:2). It was a stumbling block to Jews, folly to Gentiles, but to those who were called it was the power and wisdom of God to salvation (1 Cor. 1:21-25). Unbelieving Jews naturally rejected this. They voiced many reasons why Jesus could not be so regarded. But Paul kept insisting that this was the truth and proving his point from the Old Testament. Sabbath after Sabbath in the synagogue in Corinth, he kept arguing that the true and living God, the only God, had revealed himself in Jesus of Nazareth. He kept fervently and solemnly telling them that the Messiah foretold in the Scriptures was Jesus, and no one else (Acts 18:5).

This ultimate, irrefutable, powerful word, preached boldly, made the church in Corinth grow. It was one of the secrets of its growth—a secret we must recapture today. That same certainty will bring the same growth today. As we retrace the expansion of the early church in Jerusalem, Judea, Samaria, Antioch, Corinth, Ephesus, and Rome, we are constantly in the

presence of a powerful conviction about the only
Name: Jesus.

The church growth movement is based on solid
conviction. Christ has spoken the definitive and
final word: "I am the way, I am the truth, I am
the life. No man comes to the Father but by me."
This is the certainty the church growth movement has expressed, is expressing, and will express.
It is God's will that Christians voice it, print it,
broadcast it, shout it, and sing it. What does it
mean to believe in the Name of Jesus Christ?

To believe in the Name of Jesus Christ means
at least three acts. First, intellectual acceptance.
We move from ignorance or doubt to an
acceptance of truth: that "Jesus" is the mighty
Name—the only Name. That God has willed to
reveal himself through Jesus Christ, his Word
made flesh (John 1:14), Jesus who upholds "the
universe by his Word of power" (Heb. 1:3 RSV).

Second, since Jesus is Lord, and I accept this
intellectually, I submit my entire life to him. I
obey him in every command he gives me. He is
my Lord. I subject all my actions, thoughts,
attitudes and values, expenditure of time and
money to Jesus Christ. I treat my fellow men as
Christ commands. I try to create a family,
community, business, and state which would
please him. I accept what the Bible so clearly
says, again and again, that the whole life of the
Christian has been transformed. He is therefore a
new creation. His every act is done "in Christ."
His whole manner of life is to be worthy of the
gospel (Phil. 1:27). He is to lead a life worthy
of his high calling (Eph. 4:1). In short, the
Christian's whole life must be brought into
harmony with the revealed will of God.

A third meaning of belief is that I must share
the good news with others. Scripture says, "If

you confess with your lips that Jesus is Lord and believe in your heart that God raised him from the dead, you will be saved." If a person believes in him intellectually and brings part of his personal conduct into line with Christ's will, but never confesses him before others and never speaks of him to others, that person scarcely believes in him at all! Failure to tell others negates his assertions. Belief in Jesus Christ means at least these three acts.

We all agree that those in the early church believed in the mighty Name of Jesus. But weren't they rather simple people? Today, people are sophisticated and educated. Can modern man, filled with scientific knowledge, believe that God did in fact reveal himself in a carpenter from Nazareth, raise him from the dead, and give him the Name which is above all names? We live in the last decades of the twentieth century. Occult, mystical, and Eastern religions have swept across the United States. The sacred books of Buddhism, Hinduism, and Islam are studied on many university campuses. Some Americans make spiritual pilgrimages, leave the Christian faith of their forefathers, and journey into emergent Eastern denominations such as Zen, Hare Krishna, and Self-Realization. Can modern Americans, knowing all about comparative religions, believe that God has made a definitive revelation of himself in one person? Is the reality not that of many ideas about God, all of them somewhat true? Among them, each man or woman chooses that which appeals to him. Can moderns believe in one Name above every other name? That was credible to adolescent man, but scarcely to man come of age.

It is much too easy to assume that 1,960 years ago all men were simpletons, while today all are wise. We must not think scornfully of those far-off days. Remember Plato and Socrates, Pythagoras and Aristotle. Remember the great Egyptian scholars and the Roman philosophers. Recall the wisdom of ancient India and China. Wisdom was not born yesterday—in America. The human mind is no better equipped to think today than it was two thousand years ago. Men in the ancient world had seen many more men die and many more stinking corpses hanging on crosses, eyes picked out by crows, than modern men do. It was just as difficult for ancient men to believe in the resurrection of Jesus as it is for modern man. Indeed, it may have been more difficult.

Man in the ancient world had heard of more names of power than modern men hear, and found them wanting. Ancient man was just as skeptical as modern man, maybe even more so. But ancient man—like modern man—recognized real power when he saw it. He recognized transforming power.

The essential question for both ancient and modern men is this: Do we believe in our own reason or God's revelation as ultimate authority? If any one believes in his own reason as ultimate authority, he will not become a Christian. If he believes in God's Word as ultimate authority, then he will become a Christian. It is as simple as that. Every man has to make the choice. The marvelous thing is that as the Church makes the choice and proclaims the mighty Name of Christ, it brings multitudes to a transforming discipleship. It ushers them out of death into life. Only the Name of Jesus Christ, when held high and lifted up, will draw all men to him. Deep convictions in Christians concerning the person, work, power, and promises of Christ are bedrock for church growth yesterday, today, and tomorrow.

3
No Other Gods

In Athens Paul's "spirit was provoked within him" (Acts 17:16). The New English Bible says that Paul was "exasperated" to see the intellectual capital of the world filled with idols. Paul *knew* that the true and living God had commanded, "Thou shalt have no other gods before me." The stupidity of idol worship—to say nothing of its disobedience—annoyed him.

Today Mars Hill is just a bare rocky knoll; no buildings, no temples, no images. In the first century, however, the place was covered with shrines and temples. It, the city below, and the Acropolis above were adorned with impressive, beautiful buildings, full of idols—great gods and goddesses and lesser deities of many sorts. Paul may have been impressed by the magnificent buildings. We do not know. But we are told that he was exasperated to see intelligent Athenians worshiping these lifeless marble statues.

Paul had arrived in Athens, like William Carey in Calcutta, totally unknown. As he had discussions in the marketplace at the foot of the hill with those he happened to meet, the Stoic and Epicurean philosophers considered him a wandering "babbler." The Greek word means a "seed picker" or a "grain gatherer." Secure in the knowledge of God's authoritative revelation, however, Paul was not disturbed by their scorn. Down there in the marketplace, he continued to tell all who would listen about Jesus Christ, God's special Messenger who had risen from the dead. His audience must have been chiefly men and women of low rank.

The science of missiology suggests that missionaries should go to the top, reach for

opinion makers, and talk to kings, chiefs, and
leading men. That is certainly effective—if it can
be done. But Paul had no access to the leaders
and neither have most missionaries. Hence, they
start with those who will listen to them. That is
where Paul started. He talked to those who
chanced to be in the marketplace and "day after
day" told them the gospel.

What did he say? We may be sure he did not
attack the idols. Probably he never mentioned
Mars, Athena, Zeus, or Aphrodite. The Bible
says, "He preached Jesus and the resurrection."
His opportunity, like that of all street preachers,
was brief and limited. Paul stuck to a positive
message. He kept on telling them bits and pieces
of the good news of a loving God and his
predestined Messenger, Jesus Christ, by belief in
whom salvation is to be received. Some listened
for a minute. Some for five minutes. Paul kept
on preaching to shifting, changing groups.

Within himself, of course, Paul was tremendously offended by the image worship, the
obvious commercialism of the temples and the
priests, and the adoration of man-made objects
instead of the Creator of heaven and earth.
Engraved on Paul's mind, as on the mind of
every Jew living in the idolatrous world, were the
oft repeated denunciations, clearly written in the
law, the Psalms, and the prophets, of "other gods
and idols." Often the Rabbi from Tarsus must
have said to himself,

*Idols have hands but cannot feel, eyes but cannot see,
ears but cannot hear, noses but cannot smell, hands
but cannot feel, feet but cannot walk, and cannot
make a sound with their throat. Those who worship
them become just like them (Psalm 11:5-8).*

Paul was certain that the Athenians, all of them from the least to the greatest, ought to turn to the true and living God. The Old Testament has many injunctions to righteousness, but far and away its chief message is a command to worship God alone, to abhor other gods, and to abstain from idolatry. Here in Athens Paul, the Old Testament scholar, who could quote long passages from law, Psalms, and prophets, must indeed have been exasperated.

But the missionary cannot commend Christ by attacking other gods and denouncing idolatry. So Paul in the streets and marketplace, day after day, said nothing about the idols. Instead he kept on telling the people about Jesus the Lord. While he was doing this he came to the attention of some philosophers, who may have been in the marketplace buying a bunch of tasty grapes or spicy olives, or perhaps a juicy cut of mutton from a temple. Many temples were also slaughterhouses. Animals were sacrificed as much to get meat as to placate the gods! Out of sheer curiosity, intrigued by his advocacy of a god of whom they had never heard—a foreign deity of some sort, a bit of eastern mysticism—the philosophers invited him to speak to a gathering of their fellows. Paul seized this wonderful opportunity to expand his message in a leisurely way to a highly intelligent audience. When given the opportunity to speak to the decision makers in Athens, Paul did not hesitate. The Jews for 200 years had been seeking and seizing just such opportunities. Rabbi Paul was a professional at this business.

So it was that Paul found himself standing in the middle of the Areopagus, addressing a gathering of Stoic and Epicurean philosophers, who spent their time in nothing except telling or hearing something new. What a setting: the city full of idols; Saul, a Jewish rabbi, in the midst of Greek philosophers; Paul of Tarsus, Christ's special ambassador to the Gentiles—what a chance for evangelism. What an audience! Paul gave it his best.

Remember that Alexander the Great, the fair-haired young man from Macedonia, had conquered the world just 300 years before this. Greek culture, philosophy, gods, and goddesses had spread like wildfire throughout that ancient world. So, in the providence of God, had the Jewish religion. In those days Judaism was an intensely missionary religion. Synagogues, established in many towns and cities, were filled with proselytes. These were not racial Jews but peoples of the various countries (Greeks, Italians, Galatians, Arabs, Egyptians) who had become Jews. Such Jews had Greek and Roman names. The Old Testament had been translated into Greek so the non-Hebrew Jews and Gentiles of the myriad *ethne* could understand it. The Jews of the Diaspora were numerous throughout the ancient world. They were ardent monotheists. They remembered and proclaimed God's command, "Thou shalt have no other gods."

Jews everywhere carried on a continuous and effective warfare against mythology and idolatry. Paul's message on Mars Hill, recorded in the 17th chapter of Acts, was delivered in the midst of the philosophers in the city full of idols, within easy walking distance of the temples of Aphrodite, which were in effect city brothels. It was a well honed and oft repeated Jewish missionary discourse given to inquirers and God-fearers. As a boy in Tarsus, Paul must have heard it many times. Saul the rabbi, before his conversion, going to and from Tarsus in the towns and cities of Syria and Palestine, must have given it often. Paul the Christian missionary, as he spoke to suitable groups of the cultured and adulterous cities of Asia Minor and Greece, must have delivered it dozens of time—not to street audiences, but to groups of Gentile inquirers. And Luke, the historian, who traveled with Paul, must have known it by heart. The chief difference was that on Mars Hill, Paul had a prestigious audience.

His address, except for the last recorded sentence, was a version of the standard Jewish missionary address which had won thousands upon thousands away from idolatry to the worship of Jehovah, and to membership in a synagogue.

It is important to note the fierce Jewish intensity of conviction that God—the only God there is—is the one true and living God, and that all idol worship is abhorrent to him. All Hebrew history testified to this. Moses, Joshua, Gideon, Elisha, Isaiah, Hosea, Amos, the Psalms—all burn with this conviction. For example, Psalm 106:35-41 says

They mingled in among the heathen and learned their ways, sacrificing to their idols. Their evil deeds defiled them, for their love of idols was adultery in the sight of God. That is why his anger burned against his people, and he abhorred them. That is why he let the heathen nations crush them.

Passages like these were a vivid part of Paul's consciousness as he stood there on Mars Hill, within a few yards of idols of Mars, Zeus, Athena, Aphrodite, and a host of others.

We marvel at Paul's raw, red courage. He might well have been mobbed or beaten; he was sure to be ridiculed. This was a resistant population. He was speaking now not to sympathetic

God-fearers, but to the temple establishment, not in the safety of a synagogue, but in the most vulnerable place in all Athens: Mars Hill, under the shadow of the Acropolis above this city full of idols. The hour cried aloud for what today is called dialogue, a timid, cautious approach to those who hold convictions different from our own. Had he had the opportunity to listen to some of today's wise men, Paul might have said: "Dear friends, God has spoken to you. You are intelligent. Please tell me what you think and I'll tell you what I think. Let us explore truth together. God has given you some intimation as to the truth. He has given me some intimation of the truth. Let us share what we have." Or in more philosophic language, he might have said, "You have some speculations about the Absolute. I have some speculations about the Absolute. Let us share them, winnow them, cross-fertilize them and come out with a really worthwhile understanding of reality." Paul turned resolutely from that humanistic, relativistic path. That was unthinkable to him. He would have judged it rebellion against God—a sin against the Holy Spirit who uses God's Word to convert. He would also have termed it foolishness.

So Paul, standing on Mars Hill, surrounded by the most impressive buildings and the most profound philosophy the western world had to that time constructed, courageously spoke the truth. He was courteous, of course. He praised what he could honestly praise. He was wise, of course. He quoted their poets. He knew that the philosophers also groped for the one true God. He announced commonly accepted truths, that God had created every race of man of one stock, and had also ordered the seasons. Those philosophers while a bit skeptical about the gods, believed and taught that some power in the universe had created this orderly procession of seasons.

But then, after those kind words, Paul said clearly, "We ought not to suppose that deity is like an image in gold, or silver, or stone, shaped by human craftmanship and design."

Up to this point, in his address as recorded in Acts, he spoke as might a Jewish rabbi. This was the oft repeated and well honed speech. But from here on he spoke as the Christian missionary he was. He declared,

The Messiah has come. The new age has begun. The royal road to the forgiveness of sins has been opened by the Cross. Soon the Savior will return to judge the world. God is going to judge the world by a man whom he has raised from the dead in order to attest him as the Savior of the world. Forget the past. The days of ignorance (Socrates, Plato, and Aristotle!) God has overlooked. Now God commands (not advises, not invites, but commands) all men, Jews, Gentiles, Greeks, Romans, slaves, Athenians, bar-barians, and philosophers on Mars Hill, *to repent, believe on Christ, be baptized, and prepare for the judgment.*

The key to this message was an intense consciousness of the *one* true and living God. "Thou shalt have no other gods before me." Turn from Mars Hill, he cried. Turn to the Hill of the Skull; turn from Aphrodite to the God of Love; turn from sin to righteousness; turn from men's speculations to God's revelation; turn from idols to the living God!

No wonder the church grew. It was based on fiery conviction. Out of that sophisticated, cynical audience on Mars Hill a few believed. One, a

man named Dionysius, was a member of the
court of the Areopagus. Another was Damaris,
an Athenian lady.

Had Paul adopted the timid approach, and
chosen dialogue as a philosophy,[1] would he have
won any converts at all? Probably not! He and
the Epicureans might have had a good time
talking together, but certainly Dionysius, to say
nothing of Damaris and other educated women
of the city, would not have become Christians.

In the forum in Rome we see the same open
confrontation—and in Ephesus, the city of the
hundred breasted goddess Diana, and in Lystra,
where the idol-ridden population supposed
Barnabas and Paul to be the gods Zeus and
Hermes. In these encounters, the inspired Word
does not permit us to think that Paul was infused
with the spirit of compromise or timidity, of
joint search for "a truth which neither of us
knows." Instead we read of a courageous,
courteous announcement by an ambassador of
the one true God: God hates men's futile inventions of other gods. God has provided a way of
salvation in his Son, Jesus Christ. God commands
all men to repent, to believe, to be saved. This
was Paul's message, his gospel. He preached it
fearlessly. Stoned for it in one town, he went on
and preached it in the next. No wonder churches
multiplied.

The conviction that burned so bright in Paul's
mind has great significance for the church today.
Christians live in many university towns—
modern replicas of Athens. In today's intellectual
centers there is no worship of the statues of Mars

---

[1]With dialogue as a *method* Christians have no quarrel.
They often use it. But as a philosophy, dialogue is a
betrayal of the gospel.

and Aphrodite. Yet cities throughout America
and all other countries are full of idols. These are
not the beautiful marble statues made by Phidias,
the master sculptor. These are not altars to Baal
and Vulcan, Mars and Zeus. These are rather
symbols of self, sex, and money. The deification
of technocratic life in American and European
cities is a contemporary form of idolatry. The
worship of man's unaided reason is today's basic
rebellion against God. Romans 1:18-32 is equally
applicable to all idolatry in all cultures, ancient
and modern. Isaiah's scorching words can be
applied directly to modern cities and contemporary cultures.

A people who continually provoke me to my face
Offering sacrifices in gardens and burning incense on
*   bricks,*
They are a stench in my nostrils . . .
Because they have burned incense on the mountains
And scorned me on the hills,
Therefore I will measure their former works into their
*   bosom . . .*
They set a table for Fortune and fill cups with wine for
*   Destiny.*
I will destine them for the sword
And make all of them bow down to the slaughter
*   (Isa. 65:3, 7, 11, 12).*

"Thou shalt have no other gods before me" is
God's message for the world today. If the church
is to liberate mankind and to avoid the punishment which God justly gives to those who
deify their own concepts and worship idols their
own minds have made, the church must return to
an intense fire-filled conviction that the true and
living God has spoken. His first command is: *You*
shall have no other gods. His one way of salvation

is his Son, Jesus Christ who declared: "No one comes to the Father but by me. Who confesses me before man, him will I confess before my Father. Who denies me before men, him will I deny."

Paul in Athens was proclaiming the one Way of salvation, the one Mediator, Jesus Christ, the one sufficient oblation for sin. His courteous introduction was not his message. That was "Repent of your idolatry. Believe in Jesus Messiah, whom God has raised from the dead. Be baptized in His Name. Become a part of His church."

Until the church recovers from her contemporary worship of the cultural context, church growth will limp when it should run. Those congregations and denominations which achieve and maintain unshakable convictions will grow. Those which proclaim skillfully guarded and carefully qualified convictions will plateau and decline. "You shall have no other gods before me" is still the first command.

4
Divine Compassion

Compassion was another factor contributing to the growth of the early church. Christians were deeply concerned for others. They learned this from their Lord in whose life compassion played such a notable part. His life flowing into them produced compassionate action.

Let us for a moment review his early life. Galilee was the countryside in which Jesus grew up. He had relatives in many of its villages. While his home was in Nazareth, his father's work and events of many sorts took him as a boy and later a young man, over the surrounding twenty or thirty miles. He climbed the hills of Galilee. He walked its stony roads. He rested in the shade of olive trees and smelled the fragrance of ripening grapes as he walked through the vineyards. He probably worked tending both grapes and olives and helped in harvesting their fruits. He journeyed through the fields and drank from the wells. He came down from the hills of Nazareth to the plains, and then walked on down, down, down to the Sea of Galilee, which is 600 feet below sea level. He tramped the beaches that fringe this large lake. He ate the fish caught in these waters. Galilee was his land. In imagination we can see his footprints everywhere.

His close disciples and his chosen apostles were Galileans. Most of *their* relatives must have lived within thirty or forty miles of Nazareth. Jesus and his disciples could go into almost any village in this entire region and stay in the home of an uncle, aunt, cousin, or some family member. Let us review a few of the many incidents recorded in the Scriptures which show so clearly Christ's compassion for people.

Galilee was a conquered land. Roman rule lay heavy on the people. Palestine was occupied by a foreign power. It was one small and unimportant province in the far-flung empire of the Caesars. Roman regiments lived in barracks, roistered in inns and marched in the streets in Caesarea, Jerusalem, Philippi, Tiberius, Masada and other places. From time to time, small detachments appeared briefly in out-of-the-way villages like Nazareth. Women hurried into their houses, and boys and men watched guardedly till the soldiers made their inquiries, bought figs and grapes, drank wine and left. The soldiers of Rome were all Gentiles—foreigners—and in a real sense enemies. Rome, through its soldiers, ruled the entire territory. By today's standards it was a harsh but effective rule. Murderers, robbers, and other law breakers, when caught, were crucified just outside their villages. Their wives, mothers, fathers, sons, and daughters, saw them writhe in long, slow, painful death. Day and night the clank of armor could be heard as Roman soldiers trod the cobblestones. Some women became prostitutes, serving the army. Respectable women feared lewd approaches by the rough soldiers. Galileans hated this occupation, but dared not show it.

The entire imperial presence was supported by money collected from the Jews. The occupied country paid for the army of occupation. Romans had no intention of seeing lands they conquered become a drain on the imperial treasury. On the contrary, conquered lands fed the imperial treasury. Every soldier in Israel, every Roman administrator and tax collector, was a symbol of Rome's constant bleeding of the people, reminding them that they had to pay for the privilege of being ruled by Rome. The people feared the soldiers and hated those who collected the taxes.

When, in Elizabeth's house in a town in the uplands of Judah, Mary voiced the poem now called the Magnificat (Luke 1:46ff) she said, "The Lord, the mighty One . . . has put to rout the arrogant of heart and mind. He has torn imperial powers from their thrones, and the humble have been lifted high." In these words, we can surely see the way in which women and girls in Galilee thought of their Roman rulers. There is, to be sure, much more than that in those wonderful words, but at least this is readily recognized. From his earliest childhood in Nazareth, the Lord must have been bathed in waves of hatred toward those foreign oppressors and of contempt for their collaborators, the tax collectors.

Yet he did not hate them. Rather, he had great compassion on them. Tax collectors came to his meetings, asked him questions, listened to his answers, and became his disciples. Christ saw them not as collaborators, but as God's children. He saw them not as objects of hatred, but the objects of God's love.

One day, as Christ passed by where a tax collector called Matthew sat, he said just two words to him, "Follow me." Christ broke through the stereotype which men had built around this occupation and saw the real Matthew inside. He saw the devoted disciple, a quiet man of great ability. Christ always pierces the veneer and sees *people* with their true possibilities!

Matthew responded, followed, and learned of him. He did not enroll in a seminary to live in a comfortable dormitory while studying in class-rooms and library. Rather, he wandered with Jesus from place to place, tired, dusty, sweaty, hungry, learning from the Master. Later this same tax collector and collaborator authored the first Gospel.

When he decided to follow Jesus, Matthew gave a great dinner to which he invited other tax collectors. Could Zaccheus, the tax collector of Jericho, only seventy miles away, have been there? Could he have been a relative or close friend of Matthew? It seems possible. At the banquet, Jesus found a bridge into the lives of many despised and rejected men. We read that many tax collectors, publicans, and sinners were receiving the Kingdom of God.

Christ responded to needy people. When they were weary, hungry, thirsty, harassed, he always ministered to the needs of men and women. In many towns and villages, he must have been urged to stay as an honored guest, but he pressed on, saying, I must work while it is day. The night comes. He was concerned that the lost of Israel be found. When it became apparent that he himself could not visit all the towns and hamlets, he sent out first the twelve and then the seventy and gave them authority to proclaim "the good news of the Kingdom of God," i.e., that the King had come, and to cast out demons, and heal the sick.

Christ also had compassion for the crowds. He saw them as sheep without a shepherd. He knew he was the shepherd. He called them to become his flock.

On one occasion, Jesus saw Peter's boat drawn up on the beach of the Sea of Galilee. He climbed into it and asked Peter to push out a little from the land. From that pulpit, he taught the crowd assembled on the shore. When he had finished speaking, noticing that his disciples had caught nothing, he compassionately said to Simon, "Push out into deep water and let down your nets for a haul." Peter protested what he considered a useless move. They had fished these waters all night and caught nothing. Still, at his command, they pushed out to deep water, again threw out the nets, and, wonder of wonders, enclosed a great school of fish. The nets were so full they began to break.

The disciples were amazed! A great power was at work, and they were afraid. Then the Master Teacher saw a wonderful opportunity. Here was a vivid illustration of what he would soon commission them to do. He said, "From now on you are going to be fishers of men, throwing in your nets where men are and bringing multitudes to eternal life." The disciples must have remembered that statement on the day of Pentecost when they baptized three thousand believers.

Christ's marvelous compassion and kindness are seen in so many ways.

At Capernaum today stand the ruins of a magnificent synagogue. Those great pillars that have lasted the centuries were assembled with skill and craftmanship. The earthquakes of 1900 years have not toppled them. They were so big that conquerors could not drag them off and ornament their own palaces with them. About a stone's throw from that splendid synagogue was Peter's house. Scripture records that it was at that place the Lord healed Peter's wife's mother. Over the site of the miracle, a church was built, and then on the ruins of that a second church. The foundations are still there and parts of the floors and walls. Christian pilgrims can stand today on the very place where the compassionate Lord must have been when, as Scripture records, all who were sick or possessed of demons gathered and were healed. Jesus took on himself their infirmities and bore their burdens.

The Apostle John tells us that Christ's healings were done as signs. Yet we never get a hint that some "wonder worker" without compassion for people, was coolly arranging signs that he was the Messiah. Quite the contrary. The Lord healed *because* of his compassion. In Peter's house where the needy lay around him, he healed them because he loved them. Hundreds of years before, God had revealed through his prophet, Isaiah, that his servant, the Messiah, "would bear their griefs and carry their sorrows." Our Lord abundantly fulfilled that prophecy.

Our Lord's love for children has often been noted. Since millions of men and women have become his followers and faithful members of his Church and, indwelt by his Spirit, have elevated the lot of childhood in many ways, Jesus' compassion for little children does not today seem so remarkable. But in his day it was exceptional. We find no other religious leaders of those times nor other founders of religion saying, "Let the little children come to me. Of such is the kingdom of heaven." His compassion blazed a trail which—through the mighty propagation of the gospel—has become a high road for all mankind.

Just outside Capernaum lived a man full of leprosy. By law he had to stay outside of town, perhaps in a cave. Too sick to work, the man begged for his food. Some days he went hungry because he was forbidden to enter the town. Leprosy is a horrible disease of incurable ulcers. Fingers and toes rot off, noses decay. Such a man stood before Jesus and cried out for healing. As Jesus began to talk to him, the leper shrank away, for the law required that lepers who came too close were to be stoned. Jesus saw not a leper but a sorely afflicted brother and reached out and touched him as naturally and as easily as one would touch his own son. What amazing compassion! No wonder John wrote that even though his own received him not, "to all who received him, who believed in his name, He gave power to become children of God" (1:11, 12). Perhaps it is permissible to read "to become compassionate children of God." Certainly the best way to become compassionate is to receive Christ and to believe in his name. After all, the very purpose of his coming, foretold centuries before, was to give his life a ransom for many, to take their iniquities on himself, and to suffer in their stead. Christ's compassion became a model for his disciples, and not only a model. He gave them power to become children of God.

The road to Damascus runs through the Galilean country and along the shore of the Sea of Galilee. It was on this very road that Saul, who had been harrying the church, was traveling one fateful day. Christians in Jerusalem had been fiercely persecuted, beaten, jailed, and killed. Houses were burned, businesses ruined. Desperate fear had driven the followers of "the Way" from their homes. Christians fled from the city out across the hills. The church in Jerusalem was reduced to a pitiful skeleton. Only the apostles remained.

Persecution spread into the countryside and beyond. Saul secured letters from the high priest, and with a squad of temple police he started for Damascus to arrest the Christians there and bring them in chains to Jerusalem.

Traveling north on this road, the persecutor met the risen Christ. What did Christ say? Did he threaten Saul? No, the Lord, with great compassion, looked at him and asked kindly,

"Saul, why are you persecuting me?" Saul, in amazement, cried out, "Who are you, Lord?" He knew, but he had to ask.

Jesus might have replied, "I am the King of kings and Lord of lords. I am the Word through which everything that has been made was made." Instead he said simply, "I am Jesus." Saul, the ravager of the flock, was amazed by Christ's compassion. He had every reason to expect that the living Lord, the King of kings, would avenge himself on Saul, the scourge of the church. Saul must have been enormously surprised at Christ's kindly reply. Later Saul was even more amazed when the risen Jesus demonstrated his forgiveness by giving him back his sight and appointing him to a most significant task—to carry the gospel to the Gentiles and to be Christ's ambassador to kings!

Saul yielded himself, body and soul, to Christ. Indwelt by the compassionate Lord, the fierce persecutor was transformed into the compassionate missionary. Paul was patiently to suffer all things for Christ's sake. It was Paul who penned the immortal words "Though I speak with the tongues of men and of angels and have not love, I am become as a sounding brass or a tinkling cymbal" (1 Cor. 13).

At Philippi visitors can stand by the brook where Paul met Lydia and others and told them of Jesus. At Philippi, too, pilgrims can go into the inner room of the prison where tradition has it that Paul and Silas were imprisoned. (Whether this is the exact place is immaterial. The prison certainly was somewhere in Philippi.) The lictors had beaten them and whipped them, and delivered them to the jailer. Wonderingly he noted that the apostles were not cursing those who had falsely accused them. Then the jailer roughly fastened

their feet into the stocks. When he visited
his new prisoners that evening he saw with
amazement that they were not bemoaning their
fate. They were praying and singing hymns. Other
prisoners were listening. Whenever he had an
audience, Paul talked about Jesus. The jailer must
have listened, saying, "What a strange sort of
criminal." Likely it was the jailer who told Luke
how Paul and Silas spent the early hours of the
night. At midnight the earth quaked, the doors
flew open, and chains were unfastened.

Did Paul go right on talking about Jesus?
Probably! The jailer, too, had been awakened.
When he saw the prison doors open, he knew
his life was forfeited. He was about to fall on his
sword when Paul stopped him. What unusual
compassion! What a mirror image of the
compassion of Christ! Paul could easily have let
the cruel man kill himself. Instead, he called
"Jailer! Jailer! Do not harm yourself. We are all
here."

The jailer called for a light. Those were not the
days of electric lights. His servants had to find
and light a lamp. We can think of the jailer out
there in the dark, after the confusion of the
quake, perhaps ten or fifteen minutes, listening
while Paul, telling of him who made the earth
and sea, the mountains and the valleys, and who
commands earthquakes, continued to preach to
his captive audience. Captive not because they
were chained, but because they were hearing the
story of true freedom.

When a light arrived, the jailer—and probably
his family too—following the only light there
was—entered to see the prisoners all there. Paul,
paying no attention to his wounds, continued
preaching Christ. We read that he "spoke the
word of the Lord to him and to all that were in

his house." The jailer, tremendously impressed, washed their wounds, and at once he and his family were baptized. "Then," we read, "he brought them into his house and set food before them."

Lydia and her friends! The jailer and his household! The church grew greatly there in Philippi. It grew from Paul's compassion. It prospered because of his tender loving-kindness toward men and women.

In one of the last books of the New Testament the great apostle, who had personally experienced Christ's compassion, writes

Christ suffered for you, leaving you an example. When reviled, He did not revile. When He suffered He did not threaten. He, Himself, bore our sins in His body on the tree, that we might die to sin and live to righteousness! By His wounds we are healed. (1 Peter 2:21-24).

No wonder the early church grew. The compassion began with Christ, continued with the apostles, and can be seen throughout the history of the church. The early church recorded in Acts and the epistles was marked by koinonia. It was a loving, caring community. At the very beginning, it held all things in common. It cared for its widows and orphans. It created a diaconate so that all community members—even those in the minorities within the church—would be lovingly cared for. At Joppa a disciple named Dorcas was full of good works and acts of charity. She made and gave away many garments for the poor. She enters the record, not because of her good works (they were ordinary in Christians), but because Peter raised her from the dead. The epistles assume throughout that the saints (Christians) were doing good as a normal expression of the Christian life. They were "in Christ." They were partaking of "the Body broken for you." They were feasting on the Bread of heaven. The compassionate life was flowing into them night and day. How could they help but become compassionate?

Paul in writing to the Romans mentions Phoebe, a deaconess, who "has been a helper to many." In writing to the Corinthians, Paul praises God "who comforts us in all our afflictions, so that we may be able to comfort those who are in any affliction." In writing to the Ephesians, Paul tells them that he has heard "of their love toward all the saints." The point need not be labored. Because Christ lived in the hearts of the believers, the early church mirrored his compassion and that of the holy apostles. It was a just community because it was indwelt by the Holy Spirit of God.

Armenia was the first large country—as a country—to turn to the Christian faith. Armenia was located in the eastern part of modern Turkey, in the mountains north of the Tigris and Euphrates rivers. The whole nation became Christian early in the fourth century, but not because a great campaign was conducted there. It became Christian, tradition tells us, because of the compassion of a Christian woman. It is a fascinating story.

In a little town of a neighboring nation, about the year A.D. 260, a beggar woman carried a small boy in her arms. Both of them were skin and bones. She was a refugee from Armenia and the little boy the only survivor of a noble family. She, the nursemaid, had escaped with the child and was begging her way across the land. The prospect of survival was dim until a Christian woman took her in, treated her as a sister and

the little boy as a son. He became an outstanding
Christian, Gregory the Illuminator, who went
back to Armenia and won the pagan king to
Christ. A great people movement to Christ
developed and the whole nation of Armenia
became, and has remained, firmly Christian.
When Islam swirled around them, they remained
Christian. In 1914 and 1915 and again in World
War II, Armenians were driven from their homes
and massacred by the Muslims. They remained
earnest Christians even though scattered over the
face of the earth. Many now live in the United
States and are among our best citizens.

There is no need to recount the thousands of
illustrations of compassion shown by Christ's
church. Compassion is a normal fruit of the
Spirit. Compassion is one of the seeds of church
growth. Why do churches grow? Because
Christians care for others. The world is full of
hurting people, most of whom carefully conceal
their anxieties, fears, and oppressions. Everyone
we meet has needs which he considers important—
needs for recognition, for approval, for time, for
acceptance, for opportunities to do what he
wants to do, and for a thousand other things.
Though sometimes with a smile, everyone is
carrying a burden.

Some of these are properly carried. The Bible
tells us that each man has "to bear his own
load." Many cares and anxieties are such that the
person concerned knows he is quite able to deal
with them. He does not want others even to
know of them. He earns his own food, solves his
own problems, and cheerfully carries his own
load.

Some burdens, however, wear people down—
particularly those who feel lonely and unwanted,
whom life has treated hardly, and who have

suffered grievous loss or defeat. Even those who should be able to carry their own burdens often long for sympathy and understanding. The compassionate Christian sees his fellows in need and offers to help. He opens the door to confidences. He listens to what men and women say, ready to hear the meaning hidden behind the actual words. He walks the highway of life ready to help travelers up the hill. In the same passage where the Bible tells us that each man is to carry his own normal load, it also tells us straightly, "Bear one another's (heavy) burdens and so fulfil the law of Christ." Christian churches have always been companies of the concerned, though sometimes less concerned than they should have been. With Christ, the compassionate, in the heart, how can the disciple fail to be more compassionate than the natural man would be?

It is worth noting that if churches are to grow, compassion must be shown to *outsiders*—to publicans and sinners, to jailers and soldiers, those not in the community of the faithful. Each church must be more than "believers who are kind to each other." If Christians carry other people's burdens and help those who are hurting—inside the existing fellowship only—their churches will not grow. But if, in addition to being compassionate to those inside the fellowship, they are loving to *others* on the road, their churches will grow.

Christians in America need to remember that enormous numbers of Americans are outside the Church, outside the Body, outside of Christ. They are our own brothers and sisters; indeed, they are those for whom Christ died. Even more should Christians remember the multitudes overseas who have yet to believe. Missions is compassion in action.

Compassion is one of the seeds of church growth. This is the lesson we learn from the amazing compassion of the Lord Jesus and his tremendous concern for persons—a most important key to church growth in his time, down through the ages, and today out across the world. Why do churches grow? Because Christians care for people.

5
The
Fellowship
of the
Crucifixion

*T*raveling through the
Holy Land, Greece, Turkey, and Italy produces
somber thoughts in perceptive Christian pilgrims,
especially those committed to the growth of
Christ's church.

For example, those who visit Jerusalem soon
see that it is not a Christian city. It is a Muslim
and Jewish city, where a few Christian churches
and shrines exist by virtue of the toleration of
non-Christians. Far from growing, Christian
churches in Jerusalem exist as static ghettos, while
the Jewish population increases by leaps and
bounds. New suburbs and developments multiply,
all built and settled by non-Christians. Today
Jews are in the ascendancy; yesterday it was the
Turks, and before them, the Muslim Arabs.

This has happened and is happening in his city,
Jerusalem, the scene of much of our Lord's
ministry, the place of his passion and resurrection.
Every part of the old city, the deep valley that
separates it from the Garden of Gethsemane, the
hills to the north, and Bethlehem to the south,
bear the imprints of his feet. The paving stones in
Pilate's court—perhaps the very ones across
which the Lord walked that Friday morning—
have recently been uncovered. Within a stone's
throw of the present Via Dolorosa our Lord
went forth carrying his cross, "to put away sin by
the sacrifice of himself" (Heb. 9:26). It was here,
within a mile of the very rock where reportedly
Abraham was ready to offer Isaac as a sacrifice,
that Jesus Christ rose from the grave, "the first
fruits of those who have fallen asleep" (1 Cor.
15:20).

As visitors leave Jerusalem and travel north
through the highlands of Judea, Samaria, and the

old Kingdom of Israel, they see all around them
stony hills, finger valleys, little fields, small
vineyards, and here and there towns. In all this
land, Christians are now a helpless minority. The
new settlements built in the highlands, in the face
of stiff Arab opposition and international protest,
are not Christian. The settlers are hard-core Jews.
There will be no churches in those settlements,
and little likelihood of effective evangelism which
would leave churches in its wake. Yes, Christian
men and women think long thoughts as they
travel through Palestine today.

Further north lies the fertile Vale of Sharon,
fringed on the south by Carmel, the low range of
hills which runs northwest into the sea. There are
the ruins of Megiddo, Solomon's famous fortress.
Pilgrims standing on any high place there,
surveying the villages for twenty miles around,
see no churches. This part of Israel too is almost
bare of Christian churches.

In Galilee, his land and the scene of so much
of his earthly ministry, there are today only
sealed-off ghettos of Christians and a few church
buildings. These are the pitiful remains of what
was once a Christian land.

The bare outline of the story is this. Till the
year 350, Galilee remained substantially Jewish.
In the following three centuries, after Christianity
became the official religion of the Roman
Empire, most Galileans became Christian. When
in the centuries following their conquest in
A.D. 636-638, the Muslims harassed the Christians, the church declined. It revived again during
the two hundred years (c.1100-1300) when the
Crusaders ruled the land. Today their ruined
castles are mute evidence of that interlude. The
history is complex, but the outcome is crystal
clear. In Galilee and Palestine as a whole only a

small percentage of the population is Christian.
Most of the people are Jews. Of the Arabs living
there, less than a quarter are Christians. Far from
church growth, steady decline is apparent.

When we visited Constantinople, or Istanbul,
as it is known today, we walked through the great
church of Saint Sophia. For a thousand years it
was the most glorious of churches. Indeed, it was
the largest and most beautiful church in the
world. Then the Turks conquered the city and
reduced Christians to a pitiful minority. Today,
Saint Sophia is a dilapidated museum in which
no Christian worship is allowed.

However, a few miles to the west, in Greece,
the church survived four hundred years of
Muslim rule. The heroic Greek people did not
become Muslim. Impressive churches are seen
throughout the land, with robed priests, golden
crosses, and beautiful pictures. In these churches,
the litany is chanted in ancient Greek—alas, not
understood by most of today's worshipers. The
Orthodox Church is hostile to missionary effort
by Pentecostals, Baptists, Presbyterians, or other
Protestants. It has survived both the courting of
Rome and the sword of Islam. It is resolved not
to allow biblical Christianity access to its people.
In the country that holds the remains of Philippi,
Thessalonica, and Corinth, there is today no
freedom to proclaim Christ or to evangelize. The
acids of modernity are eating away at Christian
convictions there, as in all Europe and the West.
The flame of Christian faith grows dim.

In Athens on a Sunday, I visited some twenty
churches during the hours of worship, staying in
each place only long enough to count the chairs
and the worshipers. I found that the average per
church was 80 chairs and 12 worshipers. I was
told that on high days the churches are packed

with standing people. While the exact degree of
ardent personal faith was difficult to calculate, it
did not appear high.

In neighboring Rome, the Roman Catholic
presence was enormously impressive. We visited
the Vatican and magnificent St. Peter's, the
headquarters of the most powerful church on
earth. The beautiful buildings, seats of learning,
libraries, monasteries, and nunneries made an
unforgettable impact on us. The Catholic Church
with its numerous orders (missionary societies) is
the most extensive and long-lived missionary
organization in the world. Yet in Italy, too,
viewing the strength of the Communist Party,
secularism, scientism and rampant terrorism, we
realized that the growth of Christ's church is not
to be taken for granted. We asked ourselves,
"Will what we saw in Jerusalem, Constantinople,
and Athens take place in Rome? And will it take
place in Los Angeles, Boston, and Denver, too?"

Will the future bring extension of the Christian
faith into population after population, language
after language, race after race, and country after
country? Or does Christianity surge forward with
various tides and then, when the tides recede,
leave behind stranded star fish—sealed-off
enclaves of impotent Christians? The static
Christian minorities in Syria, Lebanon, Jerusalem,
Istanbul, and the towns and villages we saw in
Palestine, bear dramatic testimony to the fact that
this has happened again and again. Will it happen
in our cities, in our lifetime? Or in the centuries
ahead?

Wrapped in these dark possibilities of the
future, the Christian turns, as he always ought, to
the Bible. It tells the story of how, in the face of
great odds, the church grew. Piercing the gloom
like a shaft of light, comes the record of the

amazing expansion of the New Testament church.

Amazement arises not primarily because of the tremendous increase in membership. The number of Christians did increase—from 120 to 3,000 to 5,000. Then "a great many of the priests" became obedient to the faith. Samaria turned to the Lord. The gospel leaped across ethnic and linguistic barriers in Antioch. Gentiles became followers of the Way. Churches multiplied around the Mediterranean. Within 300 years the Roman Empire adopted Christianity as its official religion. The Queen Mother of the Emperor Constantine built great churches over the holy places in Palestine. Yes, the growth in membership was remarkable, but not in itself amazing. Amazement arises from three factors which marked the growth of the early church.

First, in marked contrast to the expansion caused by the missionary movement since A.D. 1500 which has spread the Christian faith to almost every land and every language on earth, God brought about the growth of the early church by *Christians* going from *"have not"* nations to the *"have"* nations. During the first-century expansion, witnesses and missionaries went from ruled nations to imperial nations. The gospel flowed from a small conquered city, Jerusalem, to conquering Rome and from a backward hinterland called Galilee to the intellectual capital of the world, Athens. What a surge of new life! What absolute certainty that God the Father Almighty was leading his church! What assurance that earthen vessels (ordinary Christians) contained a golden treasure—the divine life in Jesus Christ which must be shared with all men.

Salvation is won not by our striving, not by our goodness, not by our works of merit, but by

God's free gift made available through faith.
Salvation comes neither by being good, nor by
doing good, but simply by faith in Jesus Christ.
This faith gripped early Christians so strongly
they were ready to die for it and to obey Christ
in all things. Many Christians did die. The first
great explosion of Christianity, out from Jerusalem
to the hill villages of Judea and Galilee, took
place by the witness and unrehearsed testimony
of refugee Christians, driven out of their homes
and employment in Jerusalem by a determined
persecution. Saul, the persecutor, who had had
many killed, was at last himself beheaded. Most
of the apostles, tradition says, were martyred.

It was these ordinary Christians, untutored
men and women of faith, who spread the good
news. We read in 1 Corinthians 1:26, 27:

For consider your call, brethren; not many of you
were wise according to worldly standards, not many
were powerful, not many of noble birth; but God chose
what is foolish in the world to shame the wise. God
chose what is weak in the world to shame the strong.
God chose what is low and despised in the world,
even things that are not, to bring to nothing things
that are, so that no human being might boast in the
presence of God (RSV).

The first amazing factor then, in the spread of
the Christian faith—in church growth—was this,
that God brought multitudes to salvation through
ordinary men and women who gave themselves
unreservedly to Jesus Christ.

The second amazing factor in the multiplication
of early Christians was their absolute certainty
that God had, in very truth, opened *the* way of
salvation. These early Christians had no education,
no seminary training, no ordained ministers, no

church buildings, no philosophy, no history of missionary expansion. But they were certain that God had opened *the one way* of salvation. Jesus of Nazareth had died on the Cross, as foretold by Moses and the prophets. He was the "expiation for sin, to be received by faith" (Rom. 3:25). All your sins are forgiven by belief on this Jesus, the Christians declared. This was the good news. It was not a myth or a theory. This was the unvarnished fact. It had happened "according to the definite plan and foreknowledge of God" (Acts 2:23).

God had validated this good news by raising Jesus of Nazareth from the dead. He had been seen "by more than five hundred brethren at one time" (1 Corinthians 15:6). He had appeared to all the apostles and to Saul. Jesus Christ was alive and was directing his church. Christians expected him to return soon in triumph. They could doubt that bread was good to eat or that the sun would rise in the east, but they could not doubt that Jesus Christ had died and risen again. He had opened the way of salvation to all men and women.

Theologians who do not intend to be bound by what the Scriptures plainly say are desperately trying to contextualize[1] the message and make it appear reasonable to modern man whose thinking is heavily conditioned by rationalistic naturalism. They speculate as to what this unshakable

---

[1] The term contextualization is used in two main senses: a) making the unchanged message understandable in the language, culture, and thought forms of the hearers; and b) changing the message to make it more palatable to people of different tastes or more reasonable to people of different convictions. Christians can and ought to practice the first contextualization, but the second is forbidden to them. It creates and advocates a new religion, not Christianity.

conviction of the first Christians "actually was."
A never-ceasing stream of new speculations pours
from their pens, each pitched to a current
fashionable idea, and each superseded in a few
years by another. Though explained away in
scores of ways, the plain biblical account stands
like a rock. It is simply the most reasonable
explanation possible. God intervened in history
and did these supernatural things. The early
Christians were ready to bet their lives that he
had done so. Sensible Christians today, therefore,
follow in their steps and believe what the whole
Bible affirms. Their scholarly studies of language
and ancient culture lead them to a more exact
understanding of what the Word says, rather
than to sophisticated explanations as to why
what it says cannot be true.

Increase of churches and multiplication of
baptized believers were the products of incan-
descent belief. Nothing other than such certainty
could have multiplied churches across the whole
Roman world.

Nineteen centuries of the history of the church
records great surges of growth following each
recapturing of that certainty. Paul, Augustine,
Francis of Assisi, Francis Xavier, George Fox,
John Wesley, William Carey, Bakht Singh, John
Sung—the roll is endless. None of them would
have made a mark on history except that they
met Jesus Christ and gave themselves to him in
complete devotion and obedience. They let him
rule their lives. They submitted to his sovereign
will as set forth in the Bible.

The pages of the New Testament tell again and
again of men and women—strangers to the
covenants of promise—who, through faith in
Jesus Christ, were given access through the Spirit
to the Father. They became fellow citizens in the

commonwealth of heaven and members of the household of God. Filled with unshakable certainty that God had, through Christ, opened the way of salvation, they multiplied churches.

The third amazing factor in the phenomenal New Testament church growth was the courage and endurance of early Christians in the face of terrific odds. During the days of the great growth of the early church, the odds against expansion were much greater than during later periods when the church declined. The difference was that in the dawn of the Chrisian faith, courage and endurance were very great. Consider some of the difficulties they faced.

There was the trauma of the cross. At Gordon's Calvary,[2] Christian pilgrims may well ponder what it meant to the followers of Jesus of Nazareth to see him there writhing in agony, slowly dying a criminal's death, while they stood by, helpless. His followers stood hour after heart-rending hour, seeing his humiliation, seeing their hopes of kingdom and glory vanish. As his life ebbed away, so did their visions of rule at the right hand of power. What did these terrible hours do to them? Rome had crushed many a rebellion by crucifying its leaders. Crucifixion effectively cooled men's ardor. It would cool ours today. Yet that tremendous obstacle was overcome, once the true meaning of the crucifixion and the resurrection dawned upon his followers.

Once they saw that the Cross was God's plan of salvation—his one Way—it gave them courage to follow in his footsteps. They were enlisted in a cause so significant that "obedience to death,

---

[2] Gordon's Calvary is not the traditional site over which a great church has stood for centuries, but is where General Gordon believed the Lord may have been crucified.

even death on a cross" was seen as Christ's way
and therefore—when required—as normal duty
for Christians. No wonder their churches
multiplied. They gloried in the Cross! Nothing
could stop them—not even a Cross! All other
obstacles, all other costs, deprivations, and
sacrifices seemed small in the light of Calvary. In
paying the cost of Christian living, the believers
were simply sharing in the redemptive suffering
which their Lord had endured. They declared
that suffering for Christ was a high privilege.

The Cross was the source of their daring and
their endurance, but it was not their only
difficulty. The early church faced intense hostility
from the Sanhedrin, the rulers of the people, the
Scribes and the Pharisees. These again and again
jailed Christians. They killed James the brother of
John with the sword. They drove out most of the
Christians from Jerusalem. The homeless refugees
spread the gospel across Judea and Galilee. They
stoned Stephen and sent squads of temple police
to towns and cities round about to find Christians and bring them back for punishment.
We must not imagine that Paul's mission to
Damascus was the one lone case of this resolve to
put an end to what they considered the dangerous new cult.

Difficulty dogged the steps of the new
congregations which arose as a result of the
missionary labors of Paul and others. Paul,
writing to the Galatians, exclaims, "Did you
suffer so many things in vain" (3:4). In his letter
to the Philippians we read, "Do not be frightened
in anything by your opponents" . . . . it is
granted to you also "to suffer for his sake"
(1:28, 29). To the Thessalonians he writes, "We
told you . . . that we were to suffer afflictions."

Timothy evidently suffered grievous loss and Paul exhorts him to take his "share of suffering as a good soldier." Peter writes, "Do not be surprised at the fiery ordeal . . . rejoice in so far as you share Christ's sufferings" (1 Peter 4:12). Revelation has repeated references to violent suffering. "Do not fear what you are about to suffer . . . the devil is about to throw some of you in prison. . . . Be faithful to death and I will give you the crown of life" (2:10). Concerning "the vast throng . . . robed in white" we read, "These are they who have come out of the great tribulation" (7:14).

The amazing growth we have noted was of the fellowship of the Crucifixion. Terrible suffering did not stop it. Rather, it validated Christians as Christ's Body. When the salvation of men cost God the agony of Calvary, Christians counted it a privilege to share in that suffering. It united them with their crucified and risen Leader.

The church grew, not because growth was easy, but because filled with intense conviction, the power of the Holy Spirit, and love for God, ordinary men and women overcame tremendous obstacles to tell others about the Savior. Christians surmounted racial and cultural barriers to plant new colonies of heaven in many populations to which their businesses and their journeys led them.

We remember the great tides of history which, in so much of the Near East, have erased the church, or left small pockets of isolated Christians. Let us now consider the tides of contemporary history which, as they ebb and flow in our modern world, give us cause for concern. What shall we say about them?

First, note that the religion of Islam would never have been born if, during the three centuries when Christianity was the official religion of the Roman Empire (313-613), Arabia had been vigorously evangelized. During those 300 years only a few tribes in Arabia had become Christian. Most of the Arabian tribes were pagan, ready for change, and *winnable.* But they were not won. Consequently, when Mohammed burst upon the scene in 622, the animistic tribes became Muslim and swept out of the desert to overrun the birthplace of the Christian religion. When God, in his providence, turns people winnable and receptive, God's obedient servants ought joyfully to evangelize and disciple them. The tragedy of Arabia must not be repeated.

Obstacles to the evangelization of the rest of the world must not stop Christians today. The early Christians overcame far greater obstacles. *Given firm conviction, the indwelling of the Holy Spirit, and endurance born of being comrades of the Cross, we Christians must make sure the gospel is proclaimed at home and abroad with ceaseless, fervent faith.*

Christians are not called to beds of ease. Our churches must find ways to evangelize their cities and countrysides. The children in them must grow up Christian, not pagan, followers of the crucified and risen Lord—not of sex symbols, bank accounts, or fleeting ideologies. If we do not do this—do not effectively evangelize our land and other lands—we can be certain that the great evil forces arrayed against the household of God will triumph. The Holy Land, the Near East, and Turkey stand as vivid reminders that "we must work the works of him who sent me, while it is day; night comes, when no one can work" (John 9:4).

Second, we must recognize that the opportunities for the spread of the gospel were never

brighter than they are today. The early church
not only had courage and tremendous endurance,
they also evangelized receptive peoples. For
twenty years they concentrated on the Jews. For
another twenty years they concentrated on the
receptive Gentile fringes of the synagogue
communities, planting hundreds of churches.
Today in America and around the world, we also
must *seek out receptive communities* — they are
legion — and multiply churches and Christians in
them.

Sometimes a community which seems hostile is
actually quite receptive. It is hostile only to a
form of evangelism which does not speak to
them. The Navaho nation is a case in point. It
has been extensively missionized and evangelized,
but without much effect. Recently, by proclaiming the gospel in the Navaho language and
thought forms, and by adapting it to their felt
needs, more than a hundred new churches have
been established. In Canada between 1969 and
1979, the Alliance Church has planted more than
a dozen Chinese congregations. It found that
instead of being stolidly indifferent to the
Christian faith, Cantonese-speaking Chinese
were in fact quite responsive. Had they been
evangelized in Mandarin or English, they would
not have been won, but invited to become
disciples of Christ in Cantonese and Cantonese/
English congregations, they accepted the Savior.
Other examples from the Arab, Hispanic, and
other minorities could easily be given.

*The great evangelization of ethnic minorities in this
country awaits similar application of Paul's principle:*
"To the Jews I became as a Jew in order to win
Jews. . . . to those outside the law, I became as
one outside the law . . . that I might win those
outside the law . . . I have become all things to

all men that I might by all means save some"
(1 Cor. 9:19-22 RSV).

Christian congregations and denominations in
the United States and around the world stand
before numerous open doors. God's command is:
"Enter them." A perceptive journey through Asia
Minor and Palestine will remind us that if, like
the church in Ephesus, we lose our first love, we
ourselves may be left as sealed-off pockets of
Christians in a hostile world.

Third, in this real world of great opportunity
and great danger, growth requires constant labor.
The forces of evil are active. It is always easier to
decline than to grow. The growth of the church
never occurs automatically. Lost sheep are not
found by those who recline on beds of ease.

The only hope of avoiding encapsulation and
stagnation is unceasing evangelism focused on
saving people and propagating the gospel.
Christians must hold every yard of territory
gained. The winning football team, after a forty-
yard gain, tries desperately to gain forty more.
The static denomination which regards a ten-
thousand-member loss with gratitude that it was
no larger, is on the way to the status of the
stranded starfish.

By contrast, growing congregations and denominations are those which, after a 10 percent
increase plan to liberate even more the next year.
Growth is normal. In a world where three billion
have yet to believe, efforts at growth are instances
of faithfulness to God. The easy doctrine that
looking after existing Christians and slightly
declining congregations is all that God requires of
us is comfortable—and deadly. It must be
replaced by the biblical exhortation to work
while it is yet day.

Fourth, we should determine that, following

the example of the New Testament Christians who were absolutely sure of their ultimate goal, we will not be stopped by obstacles, failures, and high costs. The Lord tells us again and again that he came that the world might believe and be saved. God sent his only Son that "whosoever believes in him should not perish but have everlasting life . . ." Jesus Christ sends us out to do his work. "As the Father sent me, so send I you. . . . Go, disciple the nations . . . I am with you to the end." This gospel must be preached to all people and tribes on Planet Earth and then will the end come. To harmonize our wills with the unswerving purpose of God is our goal. World evangelization is our program. The discipling of all *ethne* is our resolute purpose.

We face a complex social order, a pluralistic world. A difficult task confronts us. Christians and churches from one stratum of this social order usually find it difficult to evangelize individuals and societies of another. The Christians of Jewish background did not evangelize the Gentiles easily. It took a special revelation of God and special messengers like Paul and Barnabas to lead a few Hebrew Christians to "speak the Word" to the Gentiles. Substantial barriers face upper middle-class churches when they evangelize lower-class neighborhoods and, even more, when they evangelize neighborhoods of different ethnic and linguistic hues. But these barriers are not as formidable as those faced by John, Paul, Philip, Peter, and Barnabas. Difficulties did not stop them and today are not going to stop the fellowship of the Crucifixion.

If one plan fails—if God does not bless it to the salvation of lost men and women and the multiplications of cells of his Body—Christians devise new plans. We will not turn back.

A great winnowing is going on in North
America. God is separating the wheat from the
chaff. The wheat he will take to his granary. The
chaff he will burn. It will be seen whether
congregations and denominations turn to evangelism and church growth as a fad of the early
eighties or, in faithful obedience to God's
unswerving purpose, endeavor to save lost
mankind. Those who try out a few ideas read in
a book or heard at a seminar, and then settle
back comfortably, saying, "We gave it a good try,
but it really doesn't work," are, we fear,
classifying themselves as chaff. Christians who
evangelize faithfully, liberate the captives, and
help churches grow are blessed by God and are a
blessing to multitudes. They are precious wheat.
Christians who form an iron-clad resolution to
let no plan, no humiliation, and no obstacle deter
them from doing God's will are part of the
fellowship of the Crucifixion. They will be
obedient to death and God will give them the
crown of life.

Resolute Christians are not going to be stopped
by failures and high costs. These obstacles are
there to be surmounted. Road blocks are there to
be circumvented—or dynamited. A movement
started by the Crucifixion cannot be stopped by
inconveniences. As in *Pilgrim's Progress*, lions in
the way deter the faint-hearted, but sturdy
pilgrims walk right past the lions—and find them
chained.

Church growth that anticipates quick, painless
advances will stumble easily and fall short, but
church growth ready to pay the price will win
through. If some of our programs in evangelism
do not succeed, we follow them with others
better suited to our friends and neighbors,
programs that God does bless. If our present

missionaries do not multiply churches we shall retrain them, or send out others who will. If our old missionary societies turn from evangelism and church growth, we will organize new missionary societies which will focus steadily on these essential activities. We will not *substitute* good deeds for sinner-converting, church-multiplying evangelism. We will do the latter and as much of the former as possible. We are not out for an afternoon stroll, to turn back when it begins to rain. Through rain or shine, wind or storm, sorrow or death, we are going to carry the good news of God's plan of salvation to all men. We have resolved to pay the price, today, tomorrow, this year, next year, as long as the Lord keeps us in this world! We belong to the fellowship of the Crucifixion.

6
The Mandate to Make Disciples[1]

Was the early church
conscious of a mandate to make disciples? Or
did its phenomenal growth spring from other
causes? Did the Lord command his followers to
preach the gospel to the whole creation and
bring all the world to faith and obedience? As
we answer these questions, let us look briefly at
the three main surges of growth and formulate
our answers in the light of what happened.

First: about A.D. 30-46 came the explosive
growth in Jerusalem, Judea, and others parts of
Palestine, as the Christian movement surged
through the common people of the land, in cities
and across the countryside.

---

[1] The three thousand on Pentecost and the tens of
thousands in the decades which followed did not
immediately become perfect Christians. They had not
been taught all things, but they had been discipled. They
were followers of Christ. Ananias and Sapphira were of
that company. In those days Christians "spake the word
to none but Jews." They had a regrettable degree of racial
exclusiveness. But they were disciples. They had been
discipled. We use the verb "disciple" in this primary
biblical sense. The great commission is a mandate to *enroll*
believers in churches, to *start* them on the journey out of
Egypt to the Promised Land. It is necessary to emphasize
this because in the seventies it became popular to use the
verb disciple to mean "make existing Christians into
highly educated and committed Christians." Certainly it is
desirable that Christians grow in grace and knowledge of
the Lord. Certainly post-baptismal nurture and instruction
is beneficial. Certainly freshmen in college should graduate
with a bachelor's degree after four years of study. But the
primary meaning of the verb "disciple"—to bring men to
belief in Jesus Christ and to baptism in the Triune
Name—must not be wiped out by the obvious need to
"teach them all things." We cannot hold that until they
have been taught *all* things, they have not been discipled
at all. In this volume, therefore, we use the verb
"disciple" in its primary sense: to bring men and women
to saving faith in Jesus Christ and to membership in
his Body through baptism in his name.

Second was a brief period from about the year 45 to the year 64 or thereabouts. During this period the Christian faith spread around the Mediterranean Sea, through the synagogue communities and their Gentile fringes, the devout persons and their relatives. Wherever there was a synagogue, a church was likely to form close by. Jews, proselytes, and devout persons heard the gospel, believed in Jesus Christ, repented of their sins, were baptized, and formed Christian congregations.

Soon congregations were found not only in Antioch, but in Lystra, Derby, Iconium, Antioch of Pisidia, Ephesus, Philippi, Thessalonica, Berea, Athens, Corinth, Rome, and many other places. The New Testament does not record it, but we know from history that churches multiplied in Alexandria and other cities in the delta of the Nile. We glimpse the magnitude of the spread when we read what Paul writes in his letter to the Romans: "Now since I no longer have any room for work in these regions, I am planning to go to Spain" (Romans 15: 23, 24). Practically all the synagogue communities in Macedonia, Greece, and Asia Minor had heard the gospel. In most of them, or in their Gentile fringes, congregations had formed. Churches had also been established in some towns where there were no synagogues, one notable example being Philippi. Tremendous church growth took place during this second period.

After the mid-sixties, so many uncircumcised pig-eaters had become Christian that "to confess Christ and be baptized in his name" to Jews meant joining a Gentile community. Accessions from the Jewish community diminished or ceased. In the year 70, the fall of Jerusalem also heightened Jewish resistance to what increasingly appeared a foreign movement. The book of Acts records one part of the spread, that connected with the Apostle Paul, but similar spread must have been going on in Egypt, Mesopotamia, Cyrene, and other provinces.

A third growth explosion of the church lasted from about 64 through the next two hundred years. When Paul arrived in Rome (Acts 28) he found a Christian congregation in the port city of Puteoli, and other congregations in the capital itself. In Romans 16:1-16, we find a long list of Christians living in Rome, to whom Paul, writing from Corinth, sends greetings. Their names are arranged in seven groups. Together they made up "all God's beloved in Rome" (Rom. 1:7). The house church which Paul mentioned explicitly met in the home of Aquila and Priscilla. He also extended greeting to six other clusters of Christians. It is hard to avoid the hypothesis that there were several, possibly seven, house churches in Rome.

From those small beginnings, Christians increased until there were churches in the army, among the plebians, in the houses of the patricians, and among the foreign enclaves in the capital. Christians also multiplied in most provinces of the Empire—Egypt, Syria, Mesopotamia, Libya (Cyrene), Spain, Southern Gaul, and even faraway Britain. The Emperor began to envision Christians as a threat to himself and the Empire. Persecutions followed from time to time. Martyrs in the Colosseum are evidence of a Christian movement sufficiently great to excite the anxiety and animosity of the rulers. Throughout this third period the faith grew by leaps and bounds.

Why did the early church increase in this striking way? Why did Christians spread their faith? Why did the church break out of its Jewish chrysalis and multiply among the despised Gentiles? Why did it increase until it encircled the Mediterranean Sea? Why did the church expand eastward to Mesopotamia and southeast to India? How do we answer these questions?

Some scholars reply that it was the power of the Resurrection. The crucified Messiah had demonstrated that he was alive by displaying himself to his apostles. He said, "Put your finger here, and see my hands, and put out your hand, and place it in my side; do not be faithless, but believing" (John 20:27).

Of course, the Resurrection played a significant part, but why did Christians believing in the resurrected Messiah *not* become super-Zealots, make all the Zealots Christian, sweep in many nationalistic Scribes and Pharisees, and try at least to throw the Romans into the sea? The only sufficient reason is that the Lord had maintained that his kingdom was not of this world and had commanded Christians to disciple *panta ta ethne*. This mandate was bright in their minds.

Some scholars answer that it was the power of the Holy Spirit. In *Pentecost and Missions*, Dr. Harry Boer argues that the early Christians were unconscious of the mandate to evangelize, and that the Holy Spirit, revealing new truth about which Jesus the Lord had not spoke, led them out to great evangelism. Of course, the Holy Spirit leads, but again, one must ask, if there were no mandate to disciple, no memory of their Lord's call to *all* who labor and are heavy laden, no repetition of his repeated declarations that the lost must be found and folded, how would Christians distinguish between their own desires and those of the Holy Spirit? How could they test the spirits? This was a burning question for the early church. Paul instructed them to test the spirits to make sure that the leading—the feeling that God was calling them to such and such tasks—was that of the Holy Spirit. Yes, the Holy Spirit certainly played a part, but always in furtherance of what the Word-made-flesh had said and done. The repeatedly revealed and clearly stated purpose of our Lord to spread the good news was what the Holy Spirit furthered.

It is incredible that our Lord would send his followers out upon a mission and not tell them what they were to do. He named them apostles—i.e., those *sent* with a commission. Jesus himself, we read, is "the apostle and high priest of the religion we profess" (Heb. 3:1 NEB). He was sent by God. He spent his life in mission. He called disciples for mission and trained them in mission. How could they have *not* known what this mission was? The Holy Spirit, the great Enabler, gave them the power to carry out the mission which Christ had committed to them. The Lord Jesus specifically told them to wait for the Holy Spirit because he would give them power to be witnesses in Jerusalem, Judea, Samaria, and the uttermost parts of the world. The Holy Spirit gave them power, but the Lord Jesus had already given them the mandate to grow.

A factor which undoubtedly played a part in church growth was the testimony of miracles—the lame man at the Gate Beautiful, Dorcas, Aeneas, the slave girl in Philippi, and on and on. Acts 5:14-16 is particularly impressive. Miracles and signs certainly played a part. Yet we doubt that they were a chief reason for the astonishing growth.

Some scholars attribute the remarkable growth

to belief in the second coming of the Lord. To
their relatives and friends Christians were saying,
"The Lord Jesus is returning in power and you
had better be on his side, for the day of the Lord
is coming very soon." This conviction certainly
played a part in the spread of the faith, but by
itself, it is an inadequate cause for the tremendous growth of the church.

These four reasons, each by itself or all
together, could equally well have produced a
band of Zealots, intent on overthrowing the
Romans. What, then, did cause this unceasing
witness to God's eternal purpose to save men
through faith in Jesus Christ? And what caused
the resulting tremendous growth? The key is
found in Scripture.

In numerous passages, Scripture tells us why
the church grew. The Lord Jesus displayed
himself as the Savior of the world. He intended
for his Church to proclaim him as the universal
Savior. He intended for Christians to be his
witnesses. Again and again, in many ways, he
explained carefully who he was. As the
implications of these tremendous revelations
became clear to his followers, they were
compelled to spread the good news of the Way—
the only Way—of salvation. They were compelled to call men and women to become his
disciples. Consider his words in John 11:25: "I
am the resurrection and the life . . . whoever . . .
believes in me shall never die." Some modern
Christians explain away these words. Some
maintain that they were mere hyperbole. Some
see in them a later invention of "the unknown
author of John," who was using "Greek cate-
gories of thought" to commend the Lord to
non-Jewish people. Still others "explain" these

words as a skillful attempt to put into simple language a dialectical truth which cannot logically be stated.

Unless we accept one or more of these desperate expedients (which, in making Scripture acceptable to rationalistic naturalism, destroy its authority), we see at once that our Lord is again declaring that he is the one Way. No one else has ever even claimed to be "the resurrection and the life." The good news is that whoever believes in him will never die. Again and again in a hundred different ways the inspired writers set forth the one message about the one Savior, and the one Way of salvation, and the only Way to eternal life. According to the Bible, Jesus Christ is that one Way.

There is no other Savior. No man, no guru, no sage, no potentate, no teacher, no priest, no philosopher, no one under the wide expanse of sky, from east to west in any continent, in any country can give eternal life. The word is clear: "God has given us eternal life and this life is in his Son. He who has the Son has life; he who has not the Son has not life" (1 John 5:11, 12). This is indubitably true. *It must be told to all men.* All must be given a chance to hear, believe *become his followers*, and live.

If the reader knew beyond the shadow of a doubt that a hydrogen bomb was soon going to fall on his city and nothing could prevent it, but there was one certain way of escaping it, he would tell his loved ones and friends of that way with intense conviction. The early Christians had convictions like that about Jesus Christ, the Way, the Truth, and the Life. With that same intensity they proclaimed the gospel and persuaded men to escape from the wrath to come.

Inherent in being saved was that the redeemed

share the good news. Being a Christian meant worshiping God; it meant doing good to all men, especially those of the household of faith. It meant expecting the Lord to return. It meant sins forgiven. But above and beyond these, it meant telling people that the Savior had come—that eternal life was theirs by believing in him—that believing gave them the right to become children of God. This mandate inherent in so much of what the Lord Jesus taught and said, motivated the early church and lit in it an unquenchable fire to spread the good news, to multiply cells of the redeemed.

In additon to *knowing* that belief in Jesus Christ was the certain way to forgiveness of sins and the blessed life, the command of their Lord was ringing in their ears. He had not left them with inferences from his sayings. He gave them clear commands. This gospel must be preached. Go disciple *ta ethne*; if they do not receive you, hurry on to the next town. In that day, it will be more tolerable for Sodom than for those who reject the message. God will accept *all* those who accept me. To as many as received him gave he the right to become children of God.

Imbedded in these words is the truth that the gospel is for all: Jews, Samaritans, Gentiles, slaves, free men, barbarians, Scythians—for every one! The universal Savior speaks. All men in all nations must obey and acknowledge him on penalty of being denied entrance to eternal life.

Another illustration is Christ's beautiful word in Matthew 11:28, "Come to me, all you who labor and are heavy laden, and I will give you rest." Come to me, you peasants, you laborers, you Jews, you Gentiles. Come to me, Cornelius. Come to me, Ethiopian eunuch. Come to me, red, yellow, black, and white. Come to me from

the ends of the earth. I will give you rest. There
is no narrowness here, no racial bias. The Savior
of the world, hands outstretched, invites *all
people everywhere* to come, take his yoke on them,
learn of him and find rest. This saying was
common knowledge among Christians. Why did
the church grow? Because they were proclaiming
a Savior who said, "Come unto me, all you who
labor."

Many other tremendous affirmations were
made by Jesus Christ during his Galilean
ministry. The record is full of them. While he
was preaching in the villages and towns of Galilee
he said,

*All things have been committed to me by my Father.
No one knows the Son except the Father, and no one
knows the Father except the Son,* and those to
whom the Son chooses to reveal him (*Matthew
11:27 emphasis added*).

Here again the inference from this passage,
from these words of Jesus, carries the same essential meaning as the various versions of the Great
Commission. That is why I have underlined the
last ten words. No one knows the Father—not
Augustus Caesar, not Herod, not Alexander the
Great, not Socrates, not Moses, not David, not
Buddha, and not the philosophers and wise men
of the twentieth century, either. "*No one*: except
to those to whom the Son chooses to reveal
him." No wonder the refugee Christians, fleeing
Jerusalem in terror, went everywhere (Acts 8:4)
preaching the gospel. If anyone believed, Jesus
would come in to sup with him and would reveal
the Father to him. That was *the only way anyone
could know the Father.*

In his Judean ministry, we read, "This gospel will be preached throughout the whole world as a testimony to all nations, and then will the end come" (Matthew 24:14). The clear goal was "the gospel preached to all nations," throughout the *whole* world.

The gospel was going to be—and is going to be—proclaimed by Christians. That is their unique task. No one else can possibly do it. On the mountain in Galilee, he who had authority over everything in heaven and on earth, commanded them to disciple all ethnic units. That mandate drove them out. From that time to this, that mandate has helped Christians perceive whether it was the Holy Spirit speaking or their own desires. The Holy Spirit always directed and always will direct in line with this command. The unholy spirit always leads men to doubt the Great Commission and to throw themselves into enterprises of self-aggrandizement.

Another version of the Great Commission was given after the Lord's Supper in the upper room. In his high priestly prayer the Lord Jesus said, "Father, you have given your son authority over all men to give eternal life to all that you have given to him"; and again, "I am praying for all those who will believe in me through their message . . . that the world may believe that you sent me"; and again, "Yes, Father, that the world may realize that you sent me." The quotations are from Phillip's paraphrase. These words, told a thousand times to the New Testament churches, rang in the ears of Christians throughout their lives, guiding them on and on. They had been sent *to the world* that *the world* might believe. The Son has been given authority over *all* men to give eternal life to *all who believed*. This Johannine version of the Great Commission is as clear as that in Matthew 28, that Christians are to *spread the faith.*

In addition to the words spoken by Christ in the days of his flesh, there are those spoken in the interim after his Resurrection and before his Ascension. For example, in Luke 24 we read that when he was walking with the disciples, he said that repentance and forgiveness of sins should be preached in his name to all nations, beginning with Jerusalem. There it is again, clear orders to tell everyone the good news of the only way of salvation, the one mighty Name by which men can be saved.

In John 20:21, 23, we read, "As the Father has sent me, even so I send you. . . . If you forgive the sins of *any*, they are forgiven." What power! What authority! These words were marching orders for the early church. They were repeated thousands of times by apostles, evangelists, and ordinary disciples. Christians were certain that the Lord had sent them into the world to proclaim repentance and forgiveness of sins to all and to make disciples of "panta ta ethne." The words "ta ethne" (in Matthew 28:19 and throughout the New Testament, commonly translated "nations") should be rendered as "classes," "groups," "castes," "tribes," or "clans." The command was to make disciples of all the different ethnic, linguistic, and social units of the Gentiles, i.e., of mankind out beyond the tribes of Israel.

The passion of our Lord to save men saturates the New Testament. To tell of the Savior is the main thrust of the biblical record. Our argument is not anchored to a few proof texts; rather, this is the main burden of the whole New Testament—spread the faith!

Every one of the Gospels was written that Jesus Christ might be known, loved, believed, and obeyed. All the Gospels were used to achieve two purposes: first, that congregations devoting "themselves to the apostles' teaching and . . . the breaking of the bread" might know more of Christ; and second, and at least as important, that unbelievers, both Jews and Gentiles, might hear of the only Way by which people may come to the Father and thus be saved. The Fourth Gospel, in the twentieth chapter and thirty-first verse, states this second purpose explicitly *as if it were the only purpose*: "These are written that you may believe that Jesus is the Christ, the Son of God, and that believing you may have life in his name."

Obviously the Gospels were written that those who do *not* yet believe, might do so. These are written so you multitudes (for whom Christ died but who have not yet heard or have not yet made up your mind) may believe that Jesus is the Christ, the Son of God, and that believing, you may have life. The Gospels are versions of the Great Commission, writ large. They are evangelistic tracts intended to be read *and proclaimed* throughout all the earth. In addition, of course, they were used by believers to strengthen their own faith.

Only the regrettable ingrown nature of so many contemporary congregations and denominations, and of the scholarly community which serves them and is supported by them, makes it possible for some Christian thinkers to exposit the New Testament Scriptures as if they were written for congregations which need have no missionary passion in order to be genuinely Christian.

All of the passages of Scripture we have been

quoting and many others prove such truncated exposition incorrect. It misses the main point of the life and teaching of our Lord and of the Apostle Paul. The eighth, ninth, and tenth chapters of First Corinthians are particularly clear on this point. Since these chapters exhibit a most important characteristic of Paul's whole life, we explain them at some length. In effect, Paul here (as he answers a question about eating meat) says, "Passion to spread the gospel, win converts, multiply churches, and disciple both Jews and all other ethnic units is a mainspring of my life. *It should be of yours also.*"

Ingrown congregations and denominations never emphasize the underlined phrase. They interpret these chapters to mean that Paul is simply answering a question which was troubling the Corinthian Christians as to eating meat offered to idols. He was, of course, answering their questions. Superficially, that does appear to be the primary purpose of these chapters. Yet observe Paul's answers. Though he grants that idols are *nothing*, he writes: "Do not eat meat offered to idols" (10:29); "You cannot drink the cup of the Lord and the cup of demons" (10:21); "I will never eat meat" (8:13). The tenor of the whole argument is, Do not eat meat offered to idols, *because you may cause someone* (possibly a weak Christian, possibly a non-Christian) *to stumble, i.e., to believe in other gods.*

Ingrown congregations and denominations in America seldom see the evangelistic passion which underlies these three chapters. Static-minded Christian thinkers read these chapters and conclude that the primary purpose of Paul's writing was to advise Christians in Corinth about their ethical conduct. A more correct interpretation is that Paul's primary purpose was to warn against (indeed to forbid) conduct which might cause weak Christians to believe that there were other gods, or might cause pagans to continue believing in other gods and thus fail to believe in Jesus Christ and be saved.

What do static-minded Christians do with the many sentences and phrases which speak of Paul's determination to be all things to all men *so that he might by any means save some*? They interpet them as follows: Paul, the great apostle to the Gentiles, was indeed consumed with a passion to evangelize, but that has nothing to do with us. We are not apostles. We should be good Christians, no doubt, but are not called upon to make ourselves the slaves "of all in the hope of winning as many converts as possible" (1 Cor. 9:19 Weymouth). Fortunately the text will not support any such truncated interpretation. Let us examine it.

Paul is speaking to a position which some Christians in Corinth had adopted and others had questioned. They had written asking him to decide the matter. The debated position, deducing it from Paul's answer, ran as follows: "Since idols are nothing, all things are lawful. Further, Christians live under grace not law. Christians may therefore freely eat meat sacrificed to idols."

Paul at once grants that idols are nothing, that Christians are not bound by law, and therefore can with an easy conscience eat meat sacrificed to idols. *Except* when they are told, "This has been sacrificed to idols," then they *must not* eat it (10:28). The reason Paul gives for the prohibition is clear and repeated several times in the three chapters. The first time is 8:10-11, "For if anyone sees you, a man of knowledge, at a table in an idol's temple, might he not be encouraged, if his conscience is weak, to eat food offered to idols (believing them to be real). And so by your knowledge this weak man is destroyed, the brother for whom Christ died."

Let us hear what Paul is saying. He is not concerned with justice done to the weak man. He is not passionately concerned with the petty point about eating meat. He is *passionately concerned* that the weak believer may lose his salvation by worshiping gods. And also that unbelievers (10:27) through your action may conclude that, even after you have been informed by "someone" that the meat has been sacrificed to idols, you partake of it. Consequently (so the pagans at the feast reason), you too must have some lingering faith in the gods. Thus pagans are strengthened in their belief that many ways lead to God, and are encouraged not to believe in the sole Savior Jesus Christ. You have caused them to stumble. You have aided in their destruction. Therefore, if you know that meat has been sacrificed to idols do *not* eat it. You, an ordinary Christian, ought to make the salvation of unbelievers a passion of yours and *do nothing—even a minor thing like eating meat—which may hinder the winning of men and women to Christ.*

The force of these chapters is made clear as we see the argument focused in five verses, which we reproduce from Weymouth's translation.

8:13: *If what I eat causes my brother to fall, never again to the end of my days will I touch any kind of animal food, for fear I should cause my brother to fall.*

9:12: *We patiently endure all things rather than hinder in the least degree* the progress of the Good News of Christ.

9:19: *I have made myself the slave of all* in the

hope of winning as many converts as
possible.

9:22: *to all men I have become all things . . .* that
in everyone of these ways I may save
some.

10:33: *I seek in everything the approval of all men,
not aiming at my own profit, but at that of
the many,* in the hope that they may be
saved. Be imitators of me.

The last four words cap the argument. All
modern translations make them the conclusion of
chapters 8, 9, and 10, rather than the first in the
discourse on the place of women in the Church.
Chapters 8—10 are really a discourse on doing
everything with a view to bringing men and
women to faith in Christ and doing nothing
which might destroy possible believers. While the
apparent purpose is to answer the questions
about eating meat, the real purpose is to drive
home the enormous importance of proclaiming
Jesus Christ as Savior and Lord and doing
nothing which might hinder men and women
from becoming his followers. Consequently, "Be
imitators of me" necessarily caps the argument.

The point is even more impressive when we
add the next five words, "as I am of Christ."
Christ came to seek and save the lost. On the
Cross Christ gave his life a ransom for many.
Christ called *all* who labor and are heavy laden
(in every land and every *ethnos*) to come to him
and find rest. Christ, *searching for the lost,* had no
place to lay his head and called men to be his
followers in this respect also. Paul *imitated Christ
in these matters* (as well as many others) *and called
on the saints in Corinth to imitate him.*

In the ninth chapter of Romans, Paul writes

that he has great sorrow and unceasing anguish of heart because so many Jews have rejected the gospel. He declares, "I could wish that I myself were accursed and cut off from Christ if only my brethren, my kinsmen by race, would believe and be saved." These words, written from Corinth, fit the passages written to the Corinthians which I have been quoting; namely, that a passion to win men—Jews and Gentiles alike—was an essential characteristic of Paul's life *and should be of all Christians.* In this matter (his willingness to be cut off from Christ if only others might be saved) *they should be imitators of him.* They should hold fast the traditions—the practices and truths, the actions and words of Jesus he had passed on to them—that Christians are expected to tell others of Jesus, that the Holy Spirit impels Christians to evangelize. He sent Saul and Barnabas out from Antioch and for years directed their steps. The Holy Spirit thrusts ordinary Christians out to those they can reach. Evangelization is not optional. It is mandatory. The Great Commission *in all its many forms* flies like a flag over every genuine Christian church.

Christians are to imitate Paul in his unswerving purpose to save multitudes of men and women, boys and girls, through leading them to faith in Jesus Christ. To this end Paul made himself a slave to all—*so should all Christians;* became all things to all men, that he might save some—*so should all Christians;* sought the advantage of others that many might be saved—*so should all Christians.* In these chapters Paul is saying that a passion to spread the gospel should be one of the mainsprings of the life of every Christian.

The writers of the New Testament are certain that Jesus Christ is the Son of God, the Creator, the Word made flesh, the image of the Invisible

God, the effulgence of his glory. Expressions of
this certainty are multitudinous. Bearing them in
mind, we need to read the amazing prayer of the
apostles who had just been jailed, insulted,
threatened with dire punishment, and ordered
not to speak or teach at all in the name of Jesus.
It was then that, confident that Jesus Christ had
commanded such speaking, they prayed, "Now
Lord, enable your servants to speak your word
with great boldness" (Acts 4:29).

The early church, which must have heard this
prayer quoted hundreds of times, throbbed with
conviction that the great good news of forgiveness of sins, everlasting life, and salvation here
and hereafter *must be proclaimed to all men,*
everywhere, continually and with great boldness.

About the year 31, the risen Lord appeared to
Saul as he was journeying to Damascus and gave
him a most explicit command:

I have appeared to you for this purpose, to appoint you
to serve and bear witness . . . delivering you from
the [Jewish] people and the Gentiles, to whom I send
you to open their eyes, that they may turn from
darkness to light and from the power of Satan to
God, *that they may receive* forgiveness of sins *and* a
place among those who are sanctified by faith in
me *(Acts 26:16-18, emphasis added).*

Paul refers to this commission again and again.
See Romans 1:5; 15:16; Galatians 1:1, 12; etc.

The risen Lord directed Ananias in Damascus
to confirm the message. Of Saul the Lord said,
"He is a chosen instrument of mine, to carry my
name before the Gentiles and kings and the sons
of Israel" (Acts 9:15). Ananias was a Jew and
would never have believed this was a message
from the risen Lord, except that it did fit in

exactly with dozens of sayings of Jesus, which
were current among the Jewish Christians. They
were sure he had intended world evangelization.
Saul, too, would never have believed this amazing
vision and the confirming statement of Ananias,
except he had heard hundreds of Christians
whom he had beaten and jailed say that they had
to tell others of Jesus Christ. The risen Lord had
commanded it. Now, in faraway Damascus, the
risen Lord was giving this impossible message to
Saul to "carry my name to Gentiles, to kings. . . ."

Saul simply had to believe this message so
remarkably delivered, so consonant with all he
had heard, so wonderfully authenticating the
presence of the risen Lord in faroff Damascus.
The command to spread the faith rang in the ears
of Saul as it did in the ears of all Christians. It
flew over his head like a banner. There can be no
doubt that a key reason—maybe *the* key reason—
for the amazing spread of the faith and tremendous growth of the church was that the Lord
Jesus had commanded it in many different ways,
and at many different times, and in many different places, even in Damascus!

Christians knew their task was to spread the
faith. They were to do many others things: to be
good, to be kind, to love God, to worship, to
partake of the bread, and to participate in the
fellowship, the apostolic instruction, and the
prayers; but above all, they were to *spread the
faith.* Today some Christians question the authen-
ticity of the Great Commission as given by
Matthew. But unless all these passages we have
quoted, and many more besides, are doubted,
intelligent Christians must believe that Jesus
Christ our Lord intended for Christians to spread
the gospel as a major part of their duty and
privilege.

The early church grew because of the imperative to propagate the gospel. Does this apply to the church today? Can *we today* hear our Savior say, "As the Father sent me, so I send you"? Is he still saying the gospel must be preached as a witness to *all* nations . . . and then will the end come? Is it still our Lord's directive that repentance and forgiveness of sins be preached in his name to *all* nations? Does he still say, "If *any one* thirst, let him come to me and drink"? "It is the will of my Father that *everyone* who sees the Son and believes in him should have eternal life" (John 6:40). Is the Bible correct in saying, "He who has the Son has life; he who has not the Son, has not life" (1 John 5:12)? The answer to these questions is a resounding Yes!

Congregations and denominations which hear and gladly obey these commands will, like the early church, grow. Those which will not hear, will not believe, will not obey, will not grow. It is as simple as that. The Word stands unchanged. Obedience is what varies.

The church growth movement sweeping the world insists that the Scriptures are ultimate authority. Their clear testimony is that God wills for his churches to spread the gospel. This truth must be preached . . . taught . . . lived. Then streams of living water will again flow freely from Christians, making deserts blossom like the rose and multiplying churches in every land.

Conclusion

In America the torrent of interest in church growth or effective evangelism is flowing faster and faster. Region after region and denomination after denomination is opening to church growth. Many seminaries have begun to teach courses on church growth. Several are considering opening graduate schools of church growth. Books on church growth pour from presses.

The reason for this rising interest is clear. Many plateaued or declining congregations, conferences, unions, and dioceses can readily be observed. These find it difficult to recapture growth in the midst of an increasingly secular population. At a generous estimate, perhaps out of a total population of two hundred and twenty million only sixty million are practicing Christians. A hundred and sixty million are marginal Christians, Jews, Humanists, Muslims, or Buddhists. Professor Hale of Gettysburg Seminary estimates that eighty million Americans have nothing to do with any existing church.

Many of the best, most orthodox, most evangelical denominations are also the least growing. Some of these are ethnic churches of North European background and for decades have been counting on rearing enough of their own children as Christians to assure their continued growth. That strategy used to work when four or five children to a family were common, but in the era of widespread birth control it is a sure formula for decline.

We thank God for the new awareness of today's crisis—that without major church growth (scores of *millions* of new Christians) most Americans will remain worldly people, outside of eternal life. Furthermore, unless millions of non-Christians become Christian, most restructuring of society either will not occur or will occur in the wrong direction. There will not be enough votes to change the laws in the right direction. We thank God for the widespread sharing of methods which have brought men and women to Christ and for evangelistic task forces which are being enrolled and trained. There are not nearly enough task forces, but a good beginning has been made. We rejoice in the books telling how this congregation and that stopped retreating and began to advance. Something is certainly gained when seminaries and Bible colleges multiply courses on effective evangelism and measure effectiveness by the growth of sound churches. But the time lag between teaching students now and implementing successful evangelism some years later makes us wonder if speedy enough action is being taken. We praise God for the new awareness of the terrible spiritual need of the unshepherded ethnic minorities. Yet to date the ethnic enclaves, into which a hundred million or more Americans are gathered, yield only a small trickle of conscious biblical Christians, responsible members of enduring congregations. These and other beginnings are *good*, but *something more* is urgently needed.

That "something more" is the convictional foundation of church growth. The total foundation is, of course, much more extensive than the six brief chapters we have prepared. We trust that other church growth specialists will write on other massive stones in the foundation—the Atonement, the second coming, the Judgment, the Body of Christ, the Holy Spirit, and so on. But for the time being, perhaps this modest volume will provide a biblical source of zeal in commending the gospel.

Pray to God that he will grant his churches a great deepening of certainty as to the truths of the Christian revelation. In order to grow spontaneously decade after decade, congregations and denominations must have rock-ribbed convictions concerning the one Way which God has opened through the blood of the Cross. Increasing acceptance of the Bible as the infallible, authoritative Word of God is a necessary precondition for any lasting growth of the church. The convictions which we have been setting forth, chapter after chapter, all depend on certainty that God has spoken, that what the Bible clearly sets forth is the yardstick by which all human speculations, all human wisdom, all ideologies and man-made religions must be measured. The battle for church growth will be won or lost as the convictional foundations are accepted or rejected.

Failing a widespread growth in convictions, the church growth movement will bring in only a small spurt of growth. As long as pastors pour on the pressure, membership will increase. Declining denominations will "bottom out"—and then plateau and decline again.

In much church growth writing and speaking, the convictional foundations have been assumed. "Don't we all believe the Bible? Was not this denomination born a hundred years ago in a

great revival? Is this not a highly respectable
church? Do not our seminaries give sound and
scholarly training? Our convictional foundations
are secure. All we need is effective new
methods." Comments such as these prove the
widespread but erroneous assumption that the
convictions of Christians need no reinforcement.

Such assumptions are dangerous. They mislead
us. They forget contemporary society, growing
more pluralistic and secular day by day, and
inevitably giving birth to many streams of
relativism. Permissiveness rises. It marks our day
and in scores of ways announces, "There is, in
fact, no absolute truth. You do your thing. I'll do
mine. Whether or not there is a God is not clear,
but there certainly is no authoritative revelation
to which we must all conform." Christians who
assume that we all are good Christians forget the
electronic teacher who ceaselessly, day after day
and year after year, is granted hours of the time
of their sons and daughters. The electronic teacher
indoctrinates them in "infallible authoritative
systems" which are the antithesis of the biblical.
Such Christians forget the scientism and material-
ism which are the heart religion of so many
millions here in America and in every land. They
forget that mankind at the end of the twentieth
century stands in the midst of awe-inspiring
marvels of technology: direct dialing telephones
between Europe, Brazil, Australia and the United
States, pictures of Neptune's moons on our
screens, and atomic fusion just around the
corner! What can a book written in the pre-
scientific age teach us? Because such opinions are
so common, we dare not take Christian
convictions for granted.

Literary and historical study of the Bible also—

which, when reverently used, illuminates the Scriptures—so often is irreverently used and results in the habit of asking of all passages of Scripture, "What is there about this that no thinking person can believe?"

Convictional foundations, let us repeat, cannot be assumed. In a few denominations, the likelihood at the present time is that all the church growth movement will bring them is a small spurt of growth. Then they will lapse back to plateau or decline. During the decade 1965-1974, the three United Churches declined an average of 11 percent. Such declines may well be repeated in the years ahead if the convictional foundations are not maintained and renewed. Renewal—so often a matter of feeling—must become a matter of conviction. Otherwise, lasting spontaneous growth will elude us. Convictional foundations are essential. People propagate what they believe to be eternally true. Men and women are not willing to spend themselves for what *may* perhaps be true.

Convictional foundations can be taught, whether they be marxist or biblical, hedonist or Christian. Since religious freedom is the ground on which we stand, and is enjoined by the Christian faith, non-Christians also must be permitted to teach their convictions. Thus Christians expect relativists of all varieties to teach *their* infallible dogma that "there is no absolute truth."

Claiming the same rights under religious freedom, Christians teach boldly that in the Bible and in Jesus Christ, God has revealed the absolute truth about ultimate realities. The Creator of the universe is God the Father Almighty—not a mindless impersonal force. Man is not an unpredictable accident, but the apex of God's intentional creation, made in God's image. God has given him a rational mind and free will. Man habitually misuses his freedom. Natural man is selfish, lustful, and proud. As *The Living Bible* says, "Man inclines to sin and misery as the flames shoot upward" (Job 5:7). Across the centuries, through his prophets and his Son, God has revealed his will for groping, fallen, idolatrous mankind, for the church, and for society. God has pointed out the one Way of salvation and the only Savior. His first command is "no other gods." Christ's Great Commission in a reverent summary of John 17 is: "I send you into the world to tell it that God has sent his Son to be its Savior. When the world believes that, the world will be saved." The Bible teaches these ultimate realities to all followers of the Way, and proclaims them to the millions who have yet to believe.

If secular materialist teachers may inculcate attitudes and beliefs, so may Christian parents and Christian churches. The life of the church depends on teaching the revealed truths as to man, God, sin, salvation, forgiveness, eternal life, and eternal punishment. The growth of the church and the salvation of the three billion who have yet to believe depend on Christians seeing afresh the strait gate and the narrow way which lead to eternal life, and on calling our brothers and sisters in every land of Planet Earth to enter into life by them.

In *An Evangelical Agenda*, Leighton Ford, Chairman of the Lausanne Continuation Committee, writes

In June 1980, the Consultation on World Evangeliza-
tion sponsored by the Lausanne Committee will meet

in Thailand. It will ask the question, How shall they hear—Buddhists, and Marxists, and Muslims and other unreached peoples?

It is our profound conviction that the only realistic answer to Ford's key question is this: By multiplying cells of believing Christians in every one of the myriad segments of society, every piece of the vast mosaic which is mankind. Seed-sowing evangelism is the beginning of the process. Beaming the message by radio and distributing gospel literature are good ways to sow the seed, but the gospel becomes a real option to other races and tongues when they see churches of their own people proclaiming and practicing it. Hearing the gospel must be followed by believing the gospel, being baptized and becoming responsible members of Christ's Body. *Millions of new congregations must be formed whose members go out to proclaim and persuade others of the Way to eternal life.*

Unless the convictional foundations this volume has been setting forth are built under every cell of Christians, notable expansion of Christianity will not occur. If Christians are to engage in effective evangelism naturally, continuously, irrepressibly, they must believe the following:

Without Christ young and old are truly lost; by believing on Christ and accepting him as Lord and Savior, they are truly saved. They have become, by no works of their own, a new creation. God's people have no alternative authorities, no other Scripture, no other ultimate standards of truth, no other ways to eternal life. To be a follower of Jesus Christ means desiring the salvation of others so earnestly that one will give his life—as did our Lord—that others may live.

Christians frequently rise from the Communion table, thanking God for *their own* salvation. I rather imagine that, hearing their limited thanks, the Savior of the world will ask: "For the salvation of the billions who had yet to believe, I went to the Cross. How far have you gone?" If Christians commune with the Savior of the world, how can they help but share in his worldwide purposes? In effective evangelism at home and abroad?

Convictional foundations of church growth can be summed up in our Lord's Word, "He who hears my word and believes in him who sent me, has . . . passed from death to life." Telling men *that* is evangelism—the greatest and holiest work of the church. God saves his people out of the world before, through them, he rebuilds a better, more just world. The thesis we have been advancing throughout this volume is that God's revelation of his holy will in the Bible clearly sets forth the one Way, the only Name, no other gods, and Christ's compassion for sinners. His Word also clearly calls believers into the fellowship of the Crucifixion and gives them an enduring mandate to disciple all the peoples of earth. Consequently the greatest and holiest work of the church is world evangelization. This is to be carried out in our neighborhoods, cities, counties, and nations, and to the ends of the earth. Effective evangelism resulting in church growth is the normal work of truly Christian congregations and denominations.

Part of the shining hope of today is that many denominations are now seeing this basic truth. Our Roman Catholic friends have written in Vatican II's "Decree on the Missionary Activity of the Church," "Every Christian should have a vivid realization of his personal responsibility for

the spread of the gospel." That is an essential
stone in convictional foundations. Protestants can
read that Decree with profit and will note that in
the next two pages we are indebted to it.

Evangelization is not an annual campaign to
which some declining congregation chooses to
devote itself for a week or two. Rather, it is
God's people understanding the strait gate and
the narrow way, spreading everywhere cells of
committed Christians, followers of Christ the
risen and reigning King, and thus preparing the
way for his speedy return.

According to the New Testament, evangelism
should be located at the very center of the
activities and prayers of the church, rather than at
the periphery. Evangelism is not simply one of
many parallel thrusts of the church, some of
which may be omitted. The Holy Spirit
constantly impels Christians toward the rightful
expansion of the church and the multiplication of
congregations of the redeemed.

The duty to spread the gospel devolves on the
church, not only because of the express
commands of her Lord and his apostles—to
which we spoke in chapter five. The duty exists
also because of the divine life which flows from
Christ into his followers. He came to seek and
save the lost. Inevitably all members of his Body
who maintain an obedient relationship to the
Head, will find flowing into them a great
compassion for the unbelieving multitude. They
will devote themselves to seeking and saving the
lost. The Father sent the Son into the world to
be the one sufficient sacrifice for sin. The Son
sends out all members of his Body to proclaim
by word and deed, by voice and acts, God's great
plan of salvation. This salvation is both individual
and corporate. It saves those who believe and

obey. It elevates whole communities. The divine life flowing into Christians is the mainspring of all evangelistic passion. It gives power to do what the Word commands.

The specific purpose of local and world evangelization is the expansion of existing congregations and denominations, and the planting of new ones in populations and groups where the church has not yet taken sufficient root. The chief means of such missionary labors at home and abroad is the preaching of the evangel—that Word of mighty power. The Lord sent forth, and sends forth, his disciples into the world to preach the good news. To as many as believe he gives the right to become children of God. Reborn by the Word of God, men and women, boys and girls are baptized and added to the Church, the universal Body of the Savior. Partakers of his passion to save, nourished by the Bread of Life, and revived by streams of living Water, they engage in ceaseless, sensitive evangelism.

Such evangelism constantly multiplies new cells of the redeemed, colonies of heaven, congregations of the true Church. By such evangelism God is glorified, the heart of our Savior is rejoiced, and human society is purified, ennobled, comforted, made strong for service, and thrust out into further evangelism.

Christians standing on the convictional foundations of church growth think in these terms, speak this language, express these hopes, and pray these prayers. Confident about these matters, they then try this or that method. If one method does not carry out God's will, they try another. About methods, they are intensely pragmatic. About God's truth, they believe it, whether they live or die. "For these convictions *we would die*" is their basic commitment.